As we put the finishing touches

we reached out to a group of law firm owners whose lives and practices we've had the privilege to impact over the years. We asked them to review the book and share their honest feedback—no sugarcoating, no favors. These are people who, like you, have poured their blood, sweat, and tears into the journey of entrepreneurship. They had nothing to gain by praising the book. I asked for honesty, and they delivered.

What you'll read next are their unfiltered thoughts on what this book could do for them. Now imagine what it could do for *you*.

As someone deeply immersed in both the practice of law and the challenges of running a law firm, I can confidently say these two worlds are completely different animals. The skills necessary to become a purveyor of legal services are not taught in law school and are instead mostly learned through trial by fire with many mistakes made along the way.

Charley does an exceptional job of shortening the learning curve. **His book is not just a guide; it's a manual for lawyers who want to thrive as law firm owners**. It's packed with practical wisdom and knowledge that will help you build and scale your law firm faster and avoid doing it the hard way through trial and error. His insights are **indispensable for lawyers looking to elevate their practices from good to great.**

What resonates most is Charley's clear acknowledgment that law school prepares us to be lawyers but leaves us ill-equipped to be business operators. His analogies and actionable strategies make the complexities of law firm management accessible and inspiring. **From setting bold expectations to building high-performance teams, this book lays out the blueprint for achieving success, not just as a lawyer, but as a business leader.**

Charley's teachings are **essential for any lawyer who wants to move beyond the grind of day-to-day practice and**

create a firm that works for them, not the other way around. This book is a must-read for law firm owners seeking to learn what law school didn't teach us about how to succeed in the business of law.

— BRAD SCOTT

New Orleans, Louisiana - Scott|Vicknair Injury Lawyers - Personal Injury
www.scottvicknair.com

I've been learning things they don't teach you in law school from Charley Mann for nearly a decade, and because of his insights, I'm running the law firm of my dreams. I have the freedom to spend quality time with my family while leading an extraordinary team that transforms lives through legal representation. What could be better?

If you're holding this book, you're holding a treasure map. Charley lays everything out in a way that's both practical and powerful—his ability to distill complex strategies into actionable steps is truly remarkable. Few people are willing to share everything they know about building a thriving law firm in such an accessible and affordable way.

Don't just skim through this book—sit with it, absorb every chapter, and apply what you learn. The payoff won't just be a more profitable law firm, but a richer, more fulfilling life.

— BRANDON OSTERBIND

Lynchburg, Virginia - Osterbind Law - Personal Injury
www.osterbindlaw.com

Law school teaches you to think like a lawyer. But what about thinking like a business owner? Leading like a CEO? Marketing like a pro?

In this engaging collection of wisdom and war stories, Charley Mann – one of the legal industry's most trusted coaches – brings together game-changing insights from successful law firm owners and industry experts. Through real conversations and practical examples, you'll discover proven strategies for growing your practice, leading your team, and building the law firm you've always envisioned.

Drawing from over a decade of professional coaching experience and his popular podcast 'They Don't Teach This in Law School,' Mann curates actionable advice that transcends traditional legal education. **Whether you're looking to scale your solo practice, build a high-performing team, or take your firm to seven figures and beyond, this book delivers the blueprint you need.**

No theoretical frameworks. No ivory tower philosophies. Just battle-tested strategies from people who've been in your shoes and found a way to thrive.

This is the book I wish someone had handed me when I first opened my practice. It's an invaluable resource for any attorney ready to transform their legal expertise into a thriving business.

— TIM SEMELROTH
Cedar Rapids, Iowa – RSH Legal Trial Law
www.fightingforfairness.com

———

I've been working with Charley Mann for many years now, and have been part of his Genesis Mastermind group as well. I can honestly say that partnering with Charley has been one of the best decisions I've made for my firm. Charley is an incredible coach—he truly understands the challenges that law firm owners face and provides actionable, practical strategies to help you thrive.

Under Charley's guidance, my firm has experienced consistent growth and success, even during challenging times. His coaching goes far beyond surface-level advice; it's tailored, thoughtful, and always focused on long-term success. Whether it's refining marketing strategies, improving team dynamics, or creating systems that actually work, Charley has been a constant source of support and expertise.

The Genesis Mastermind itself is also a game-changer. Being part of a group of driven, like- minded professionals has given me valuable insights, encouragement, and ideas that I couldn't have found on my own. It's not just a coaching program—it's a community that pushes you to be better and holds you accountable to your goals.

Charley genuinely cares about his clients' success, and it shows in everything he does. I'm grateful for his guidance and the positive impact he's had on my business and life. If you're looking for a coach who will help you level up your business, I can't recommend Charley Mann and the Genesis Mastermind highly enough.

— MIKE MONTEFORTE
Woburn, Massachusetts – Monteforte Law, P.C. – Elder Law and Estate Planning
www.montefortelaw.com

When an author references both Chumbawamba and, subtly, long-time Cincinnati Reds radio announcer Joe Nuxall—whose trademark radio sign-off phrase, "This is the old left-hander, rounding third and heading for home," is displayed outside the Reds' stadium—you can tell he casts a wide net.

Charley Mann is a modern renaissance man. From humble beginnings as a theater major, he has evolved into a marketing guru, podcaster, sought-after speaker, and respected business mentor for lawyers. Sounds crazy, right? You'll understand after reading "They Don't Teach This in Law School." Charley is a lifelong learner and active listener with a quick mind, an engaging personality, and plenty of wisdom for someone so young. I think it's because he's intentional about this: he listens to his clients, learns from those who've come before, and constantly explores new ideas to encourage outside-the-box thinking.

I have long heard from colleagues that many of us attorneys are poor business people. My own experience confirms this. Although a practicing attorney for many years, I knew little about managing my practice as a business. That might work for a time, but not for the long term. People who need my services must be able to find me, which means marketing. I met Charley nine years ago, and through him, I connected with other attorneys who wanted to learn about the business of law. With Charley's and others' guidance and encouragement, we have learned to enjoy practicing law again. We serve our clients and communities better and are also better spouses, parents, and friends as we learn to manage our practices instead of letting them dictate our lives. Our revenues have increased as well.

Attorneys and marketers share their stories in this book. They all started small and encountered frustration and discouragement as they wondered, "Why isn't this working?" They learned to enjoy and succeed at practicing law, perhaps for the first time in years.

My sensei and friend, Charley, has put much of his heart into these pages. His teachings will benefit you, as they have me and many others.

— JIM MONAST
Upper Arlington, Ohio – MonastLaw – Workers Compensation
www.monastlaw.com

I've had the privilege of working with Charley in mastermind and coaching settings for several years, and one thing is clear—he has seen pretty much any problem out there. He has not only helped law firm owners navigate their biggest challenges but also put systems in place to prevent them from happening in the first place. If you're facing obstacles in your practice (and let's be honest, who isn't?), this book is a must-read.

Grab your copy now—you'll find solutions to problems you're dealing with at this very moment.

– SCOTT SNELLINGS
Dallas, Texas – Snellings Injury Law – Personal Injury
www.snellingsinjurylaw.com/attorneys/scott-snellings/

Thank you for writing this book—I truly appreciate it! They Don't Teach This in Law School is a refreshingly candid and practical guide for lawyers looking to build and grow a successful law firm. Based on Charley Mann's podcast of the same name, it brings together insights from legal industry experts, covering everything from marketing and branding to leadership and business strategy. This isn't about practicing law—it's about running a law firm like a thriving business. Written in a conversational, no-nonsense tone, the book delivers real-world advice that firm owners can actually put into action.

What makes this book stand out is its emphasis on practical strategies over vague theory. Contributors share their expertise on client acquisition, branding, and scaling operations, while Mann provides a compelling framework for shifting from an overworked attorney to a strategic leader. Whether you're a solo practitioner looking to grow or a firm owner ready to break through to the next level, this book is packed with insights to help you get there. **If you're serious about building**

a law practice that runs efficiently and profitably, this is the playbook you've been looking for.

– CHONG YE
Lakewood, Washington – The Ye Law Firm – Injury Lawyers Personal Injury
www.theyelawfirm.com

I can unequivocally say that my practice (and life!), wouldn't be where it is without Charley's guidance, friendship and (gulp) tough love. It has been a privilege to both get to know, and learn, from Charley over the past 10 years. He is always on top of his proverbial game, staying up to date with all the trends and is a never-ending source of knowledge. Charley is someone that consistently "brings it" like no one else. This book is no different and just the beginning from this titan in the field.

Thank you Charley for everything you've done for my life and practice and I am happy to know that the rest of the world will also be served by you through this book.

– DANIEL IZQUIERDO
Miami, Florida – Criminal Defense
www.izlegal.com

If you're running a law firm – or any business, for that matter – you need to read They Don't Teach This in Law School by Charley Mann. This book isn't just another business or marketing guide; it's a masterclass from someone who truly understands the business of running a law firm.

Charley's passion for marketing, business, and the art of building a firm is unmatched. I've had the privilege of seeing it firsthand – his sharp insights, his no-nonsense approach, and, most of all, his unwavering commitment to helping others succeed. He doesn't just teach theory; he lives this stuff every single day. And because of that, his lessons aren't just concepts - they're game changers.

The principles in this book have not only grown my firm but have transformed my life. I'm working smarter, not just harder. My business is more profitable, my systems are stronger, and – maybe most importantly – my quality of life has improved in ways I never thought possible.

But what sets Charley apart isn't just his brilliance; it's his authenticity. He's sharp, yes, but he's also genuine. He cares. He gives everything he has to his clients, his readers, and his friends. I count myself lucky to be all three.

They Don't Teach This in Law School is more than a book; it's a blueprint for building something bigger, better, and more fulfilling. If you want to grow your firm – and your life – read it now.

— KEVIN DEEB
Coral Gables, Florida – Deeb + Deeb Attorneys at Law – Estate Planning, Civil and Commercial Litigation
www.deebpa.com

THEY DON'T
TEACH THIS IN
LAW SCHOOL

ISBN: 978-1-63385-543-4

Published by
Word Association Publishers
205 Fifth Avenue
Tarentum, Pennsylvania 15084

www.wordassociation.com
1.800.827.7903

THEY DON'T TEACH THIS IN LAW SCHOOL

CHARLEY MANN

CONTENTS

FOREWORD

THE ARTIFICIAL INTELLIGENCE BOOM has made a mountain of new authors. You can scroll through countless pages on Amazon, find countless new authors peddling promises of success, and every day it's becoming harder to distinguish authenticity from artificiality. Every day it becomes harder to spot genuine expertise among the fakes.

In 2024, intelligence has become commodified. Knowledge is a few words in a search bar, and a click, away. We've become saturated.

We have information, without guidance. We have knowledge, without power. We have ideas, without a clue. Knowledge is easily obtained today, but wisdom is still prized. Wisdom is still a luxury.

This book is filled with wisdom. This book can change your life.

When Charley approached me to help compile this collection of marketing strategy and wisdom, I was convinced I wasn't the right person. I may have tried to talk him out of it.

I didn't know the first thing about Legal Marketing. Charley reassured me I was up to the task.

I am so grateful he did.

I began to immerse myself in his podcast, *They Don't Teach This in Law School*. I listened to the prolific minds he brought on the show. I began to show up and pay attention, and something ignited inside of me. When I wasn't writing, I found myself talking about the things I was writing about, the things I was learning, in my everyday conversations. My thinking began to frame itself around the ideas relayed in the pages ahead. I began to feel this tug at the back of my mind, an offering, to become a new version of myself. Equipped with all of this knowledge, I've started a journey redefining what my version of success can be, creating new goals, and feeling equipped to achieve them.

I've discovered that the nagging feeling of being too uninformed, too unequipped, and too unremarkable to chase the things really worth obtaining isn't unique to me. Every year, people leave school realizing there is so much about their field they've yet to learn. This is a universal feeling and, in this book, there are universal solutions.

It's filled with people who stumbled, who sweat, and through their experiences have thrived. In the pages ahead, you'll find contagious ideas to propel yourself forward.

I'm no lawyer but spending time with these pages did all of it for me. Imagine what it can do for you.

Knowing Charley as long as I have, I'm confident he could have done anything with his life. I think the world is fortunate he chose the path of coaching. He left his mark on me early in life by conjuring the best from people. I'm thrilled to see him still doing it, on a much larger and wider stage. If the greatest mark of an alchemist is bringing gold from lead, there's no better title for his company than Law Firm Alchemy.

Settle in, turn the page, and come make gold with us.

—*Bryan Austin*

LIKE ANY GREAT ARTIST, I'M BEHIND SCHEDULE AND OVER BUDGET
(THE INTRODUCTION)

I'M LATE.

As in, I'm behind schedule on delivering this chapter.

But here's the good news: I have a great team to keep the ball rolling. My longtime friend, Bryan Austin, is handling the conversations right now with our awesome publishers, Tom and Francine Costello of Word Association. Together, they are editing all of the amazing contributor and "Charley" chapters pulled from my podcast, *They Don't Teach This in Law School*.

Meanwhile, my executive assistant, Ifhel Balaba, is keeping me as on track as one can keep a rabid wolverine on track. (Side note: Go Wolverines. And go Wolverine, for my fellow X-Men fans.)

And I have the outstanding Jenny Sajdera handling the full-scale operations of the business. She's making sure there's a launch plan for this wonderful tome of wisdom.

Let good people help carry the burden.

Success is a team sport.

I imagine that's one thing they don't teach enough, if at all, in law school. I hear from the firm owners I coach about their backgrounds in law school. You are measured against your peers. It's a competitive rather than collaborative environment.

Understand, my comparison point is live theater.

I was a theater major in college with no grad school to my name. Much of what I learned about succeeding comes from live theater. And let me tell you, live theater is very much a team sport. There are so many moving parts, it's hard to account for all of them. And, like a personal injury case moving from pre-lit to litigation, the team may change along the way - certainly the processes do.

The best actors focus on just being a great actor. They aren't there to do the stage crew's job.

The director is busy directing and setting the tone for the show. While they may ask for certain themes from the lighting designer, they shouldn't meddle in which specific lights are used.

And the stage manager is there to ensure everything runs smoothly. It's not his or her job to improve the blocking (how people move onstage) - only to make sure it is consistent and that cues are hit.

Everyone needs to trust others to do their job.

Because if you don't trust the other people, you won't do your job well. You will spend all your time worrying about what they're up to, and eventually it all comes crashing down. At minimum, you will hit a wall. I see this often in law firms. The firm grows to the limits of its leadership - usually right around where the leader is no longer willing to give up control and trust others.

That's my long-winded excuse for writing this chapter at the end of the process. I'm just so darn good at trusting my people. (Yes, I'm rolling my own eyes at myself.)

Fortunately, the people I brought into the process are bringing this to life.

I say fortunately, because...

The contributors in this book deserve to be heard. I suppose that statement is both generous and egotistical. After all, the book is chock full of law firm owners, vendors, and others who share their insights and experiences. I want you to pay attention to them. The book also happens to include many chapters from yours truly - the egotistical side. To be fair, I think you need an ample ego to step out and consider your words worth publishing.

This book is different from many others in the law firm support and success space.

Our goal was to create a *Tools of Titans* for law firm owners. As with Tim Ferriss's whopper of a book, we drew on the strengths of the wonderful people who have been guests on my podcast. Each one brings a different perspective and story. All are experts in their own ways, and you now have a book you can flip open to any page to gain new ideas and inspiration.

"Flip open to a page" is also our minimalist user's manual for this book.

Like Ferriss's murder weapon of a book (it is voluminous in size and deadly if wielded in the right hands), this collection can be consumed in non-sequential order. Feel free to drop in to a preferred author's chapter(s). Or read from start to finish. Your choice, my fine friend.

In all cases, except for this chapter and my co-author's intro chapter, the book is built on the transcripts from individual episodes of *They Don't Teach This in Law School* (podcast). The guest contributor chapters are intended to be in their voices. When you see "I" in their chapters, it is intended to be the contributors speaking, not me. Many, but not all, offered revisions to their chapters before publishing. Ultimately, if you see something that jives with you, I recommend you follow up with these fantastic human beings. And if you see something that absolutely enrages you, follow one of Stephen Covey's beloved seven habits and "seek first to understand." Reach out and start a conversation.

To wrap this up, I have one great hope for this book.

I hope you will take action.

I don't want this to be just another collection of ideas, though there are many. I want you to affect change in your world. The magic is in the action more than the idea. So if all this book does is provide you with the gumption to do something, our work is done. You will inevitably make the world a little bit brighter and better for taking action. I believe this because the many law firm owners I work with are exceptional people. They employ people in good jobs, care deeply about their clients, and support their communities with abundant love and energy. Our world needs these qualities more than ever.

—*CHARLEY MANN*, May 2024

chapter 1

INTRINSIC VALUE
WITH JAN ROOS

Jan Roos is an award-winning entrepreneur, author and speaker. Within a year of starting as a freelance media buyer he was working with some of the largest personal injury law firms in the country. Since then, his company, CaseFuel, has worked with hundreds of law firms across all the major practice areas and managed over $10 million in ad spend across all of the major ad networks. The practice has expanded to include conversion rate optimization, intake, and leadership training to help law firms get the highest return on their investment and scale their firms with confidence.

HOW DO YOU ASSIGN VALUE to your leads? The default way I've seen most law firms value a lead is *ex post facto*. After the fact.

"If it closed, it's a good lead."
"If it doesn't close, it's a bad lead."

It has all the nuance of a crass catcall on a New York City street.

Maybe it's reductive, but it's literally how it goes. How can we find a better approach to assigning value to a lead? First, let's zero in on the two forms of value we can assign to a lead: which is intrinsic value and realized value.

INTRINSIC VALUE AND REALIZED VALUE

Intrinsic value is what the case would be worth to anybody. For example, we have a personal injury case which, in the hands of a competent litigator, could yield a $300,000 settlement. At the end, the attorney collects $100,000 from it. The intrinsic value of the lead would then be $100,000. But let's say the intake team drops the ball. Let's say it's not appropriately qualified. It doesn't go in front of the right people. It doesn't get full use value. We end up getting significantly less than what the case would have originally been worth. **This is realized value: what the case ends up being worth to you in the end.** Usually the way people measure the value of their lead is with realized value vs. the intrinsic value of the lead itself.

It's very important to focus on the intrinsic value of people coming in. It can take a little bit of restructuring, but it's worth it in the long run.

MEASURING INTRINSIC VALUE

The first thing that you have to do, in order to recognize intrinsic value, is to figure out what represents the likelihood of a lead hiring you. A lead with a high likelihood to move to the next step is called a **qualified opportunity**.

Begin by asking, "Is this somebody I could sell my services to?" Reverse engineering the process reduces the response to a binary yes or no. The process suddenly becomes a whole lot simpler, and frees you up from any unnecessary mental hoops to jump through. It stays in the bounds of your control, from a process perspective. I'll use some of our solo clients, in estate planning, as an example. We move past all of the insane criteria and we begin with simple questions:

- *"Does this person have a house?"*
- *"If not, do they have at least six figures in assets they are looking to protect?"*
- *"Have they watched the webinar and/or consumed whatever content we're putting in front of them?"*
- *"Do they operate in a state where the attorney is a member of the bar?"*

If the answer to all of those questions is yes, then we have somebody we can definitely close for an estate planning firm. What this ends up ruling out is the bias which can often come from opinion.

- *"So and so was rude."*
- *"They said they were going to follow up and then they never showed up."*

- *"I hate the zip code they're from, have you seen the houses in that area?"*

Continuing along the process of valuing our leads, how do we measure success? Let's say we have eight qualified **consultations**. The benchmark we like to shoot for with cold traffic leads is **closing** 50%. If we get four, wow! We're doing great! If we got six, we're even better!

In my experience, even with the best attorneys you're not going to hit 100%, but 70, 80% over the course of a calendar year is totally achievable!

PREEMPT THE OBJECTION BEFORE IT'S THERE

The thing I've found, which also goes into my philosophy on handling objections in actual sales calls, is when you go into a situation where there is an objection the way to get around it, in sales or any other context, is to preempt it.

Leading with content is like a lawyer proactively starting the relationship with a client. We have the chance to say who we are, and what we're about, before we ever have a conversation with the client about sales. We get to have them foster a relationship with our work before we ever talk to them. For clients we sign, we are upfront with the expectations we set. For instance, we have every single client we sign go through what we call a "fast start session". We go over our philosophy. We tell them who we are.

We say, "Hey look, this is the cycle of mental gymnastics you'll go through, and these are the results you're going to get if you believe this."

"These are the results when you believe this one leads to success, and this one leads to ruin and a wasted investment."

"Which one do you prefer?"

You've got to be that stark sometimes.

CLEAR QUALIFICATIONS

Let's imagine a situation where you're trying a new online marketing strategy. You're trying a new traffic model. Up until now, you've run most of your ads on Facebook. You want a model of what a Youtube lead looks like. You run your first few ads, and all three come from similar demographics (income sets, zip codes, eye-color you name it).

You start creating a limited data set of what you tend to expect of these things. Make it black and white. Get the qualifiers out of the way. Be upfront of what you need your leads to be, so there is no room to waver. It helps sort apples and oranges, and keeps your basket full. When you have this stuff set up, it's the Midas touch. Every lead becomes gold. Every question becomes a yes. When you have the right structure in place, you can take absolute garbage leads and flip them into treasure.

The reality is, too many firms don't do a thorough enough follow up process. They start downgrading leads before fully analyzing why they failed. Often, the failure is actually on their end. The failure isn't in the quality of their leads but rather the quality of their process.

What's consistent through all of it is that legal issues are extremely pressing and everyone, no matter the demographic, has the full, and high, range of urgency to have their problems solved. People need your help. Everyone who comes looking for you needs your services.

BE THE SOLUTION, NOT AN OPTION

If you let it be an option for someone to hire you, you're going to be just an option to them. The easiest decision for someone to make is to do nothing. You have to meet their desire for 'easier', and you have to offer them 'better.'

You have to make the decision for them, and then do everything in your power to get them to show up. Get them to call you, sign up for the appointment, sign as a client, and then follow through with whatever obligations they'll have. You'll end up with a better ratio of speed to cash, or if you're getting paid up front, a better ratio of converting your lead into a fully realized and finished product. You're not just stacking up inventory.

A part of the journey is developing a black and white system for assessing the intrinsic value of a lead; and then putting systems in place to ensure your realized value matches, or exceeds the intrinsic value.

ALCHEMY IN ACTION:

Defining value: Understand the concept of valuing a lead; intrinsic and realized value. Ensure your realized value matches, or exceeds the intrinsic value.

Structure for success: Understand the importance of qualification, and structure your sales process to align intrinsic and realized value.

Checking bias: Develop impartial systems for valuing leads to avoid confirmation bias that could hurt qualification.

Keep the work in front of you: Don't try to close 100% of your cases. It's about growth, not comfort.

chapter 2

MASTERING MARKETING
WITH ANDY STICKEL

Andrew Stickel *is a Law Firm Marketing Expert, Author, and Co-Founder of Social Firestarter, LLC. A native of Baltimore, Stickel started his first marketing venture at age 19 in Fort Myers, Florida. After exiting his next marketing company in 2012, Stickel has served thousands of attorneys, helping their law firms maximize marketing ROI and doing what it takes to get more clients. He posts daily YouTube video trainings and hosts The Official Lawyer Marketing Facebook Group.*

BEING GOOD AT SOMETHING does not correlate to getting paid well for it. Being good at something, and marketing yourself well, means getting paid well for it. Some people might disagree, but I stand by it.

I've spoken to many lawyers over the years who end up falling into the trap of thinking that because they've reached a certain skill level, success should automatically come to them. Success in this field is two-fold. You need to master the trade of law, and you need to perfect the craft of marketing yourself. You can't have one without the other. A great marketer who sucks at being a lawyer will eventually fold. A lawyer without an aptitude for marketing will never grow as far as they'd like to. You don't need another degree. You don't have to go back to school. You don't need to be a marketer who's also a lawyer, but if you can be a lawyer who markets? You'll level up, and quickly.

Some people mistakenly assert that lawyers shouldn't have to run ads. They believe good work should speak for itself. In some respects it's true. Good work will get you plenty of referral clients, but to see exponential growth? To attain the kind of growth which lets you hire rockstar employees, deliver amazing results, and work the way you dream of working? You have to learn to advertise. You've got to master marketing.

PROVIDE VALUE

The way that I like doing all my marketing is through one simple philosophy. Prove you can help people by actually helping them. I arrange all of my ads with this in mind. **Value adds meaning.** I try to assign some sort of value to all of my ads. Typically, I'll teach something in an ad and, at the end, I'll say, "If you want to learn more buy my book, come to my event, schedule a consultation, et cetera." If someone watches the ad and takes no action, there is still value in the ad. They've walked away with something they didn't know before. I have a YouTube channel with over 1500 videos, all devoted to helping lawyers solve small problems they might face in their firm. Whether they hire me or not, I am adding value to both my brand and my business. I'm still putting myself out there.

The reality is that most people you reach will never hire you, but there is still the ability to impact a lot of lives. The people who do hire you, because of the value you've attached to your content, will have automatic trust and confidence in your capabilities. They will be acquainted with who you are, how you work and what you do.

When you actually provide value which helps people, you don't have to work as hard to sell people on your business. You can get creative and create content you find engaging and interesting. You don't have to reinvent the wheel, either. There are a million ideas which have already proven successful at selling a product. You don't have to get good at inventing something from thin air. You just have to open your eyes and see what's out there already that makes people want to engage.

FARMING IDEAS

One of the things you can never do enough is farm. I'm not talking about agriculture when I say it, I'm talking about ideas. Farming is zooming out from your industry, looking across multiple industries to see what works, and finding out how it could be molded to apply to your industry.

Observe what people are doing to effectively bring people to their business and discover how it could apply to yours. You see it a lot in the real estate industry, but it can apply to the service industry, the arts and the legal industry as well.

Dan Kennedy, probably the most well-known marketer of all time, famously said he never had an original idea, nor did he ever plan on having one. He's made his prolific career by looking across industries to see how people are selling and has applied it in prolifically effective ways.

Figure out what other people are finding success in. Determine what works in other markets and how to apply it. You have to ask, "how can these principles apply to my market?" Experiment. Fail. Learn, and grow.

Failure is part of the process. I've tried so many things which haven't worked. If I try ten things, chances are eight of them will fail and I still count it as a win. I've still gained two things I wouldn't have had otherwise. There's this misconception that marketers have all the answers. The reality is nobody knows the answer. Marketing is about testing what works and moving forward. I don't see it as failure. I see it as research. I learn what doesn't work, and what's effective. I discover the good, and the bad, by throwing them against the wall to see what's sticking.

If you spend your time hesitating, or not acting because you're uncertain, the result will be the same as if you failed. Nothing will happen. Nothing comes from nothing. Try, assess and refine. Develop your formula.

After years of trying, failing and refining I've developed a simple formula which you can identity and apply to the most effective ads in the market. The best ads are composed of a *hook, the pull* and *the call.*

FINDING A HOOK

There are a few things which tend to be consistent in ads, one of which is that if you don't hook your audience in the first few seconds, you will lose them. We live in an age of fast content, and fingers swipe faster than our brains once we get locked into a cycle of scrolling. Your message has to stand out. It has to have a hook.

One of the biggest mistakes I see lawyers make in their advertisements is wasting inertia in their opening. They'll start their videos with,

"Hello I'm John Smith. I'm an attorney at Smith, Smith and Smith. I've been an attorney in Smithsville for twenty-two years..." They start their videos with so much unnecessary exposition and end up losing their audience before the second 'Smith'.

When you look at the most successful YouTubers on the platform, you see them begin their videos with action. They begin their videos with a hook so effective you're engaged before you have the chance to realize it. Look at Mr. Beast who, love him or hate him, has built an incredibly far-reaching empire for himself with very little substance. He doesn't waste time on exposition. He just jumps right into it.

"I took ten people, put them in a private jet and lit them on fire. Last one in the jet wins $100,000."

There's the video. There's no nuance. There's no substance, but the audience is hooked. He doesn't need to say, "Hi, I'm Mr. Beast and I create crazy videos." There's no need to, the action says it for him. It might seem like a stretch to translate something like Mr. Beast into what you do with your law firm. This is an opportunity where *farming* can really help translate what works.

Rather than opening your video with introductions, try a dynamic summary of what you'll talk about.

"Are you tired of working nonstop 60 hours a week and having nothing to show for it? Here are three ways to work less and make more."

Suddenly you have a video which instantly resonates with someone. You've presented a problem people identify with, and the promise of a solution. You have the blueprint for an incredible, shareable piece of content.

In the world of legal marketing, you're not competing against other law firms. You're competing with everything on social media. You're competing against all of the noise, products and systems vying for people's attention. Finding a great hook breaks through some of those initial barriers and provides you with the opportunity to pull them in.

KEEPING THEM ENGAGED

If you can hook them in the first five seconds, the next challenge becomes keeping their attention. If you can give them something interesting enough, you'll keep them. There are two concepts I use to keep people engaged to the end of my ads. The first is called the *loop*. The loop consists of offering information at the beginning of the video, then giving the information at the close of it. This leaves your audience engaged and watching, waiting for the promised information.

For example, I'll offer something like, "Did you know there is one trick you can take advantage of to become a millionaire in the next year? Stick around till the end of the video to hear the trick, and in the meantime I'll tell you about how I discovered it."

I'm painting with broad strokes but it's easy to see the mechanics of the loop. I put forward a promise at the beginning of the video to deliver something at the end of it, and in the meantime I have an engaged audience waiting for the promise made at the beginning.

Another thing I utilize are *listicles*. Listicles are articles formatted as a list. Think Buzzfeed. Lists are a great way to arrange the content you frame between your loop. If we return to our hypothetical *million-dollar trick* example, you can continue to build engagement in the video by saying, "Here are the three things I discovered while unlocking this unique trick." Each item on the list has the chance to grapevine your message, directing the audience back to the information you're trying to impart.

To keep people engaged, it's important to know what drives them. What I've discovered over the years is people are less drawn to pleasure than they are an escape from pain. People are drawn to things which offer to help them with their problems. They tend to look at offers of money, happiness or peace of mind with skepticism. You can utilize it to your advantage.

People are much more likely to allow strangers to help them get out of pain than they are to lead them towards pleasure. When you're creating ads, if it's a cold audience who doesn't know who you are, you don't necessarily want to open with promises of a new life. Instead, you want to offer solutions to problems. A lot of people work too much and get paid too little. An offer to alleviate the burden and find a better road can get a lot of traction. It can garner a lot of trust.

THE CALL

The final piece of the structure is *the call*. It's the transition to get someone to take the next step. When we're talking about direct response marketing, it's the call to action. You want them to email, or call, or visit the link you provide. You want them to engage further.

When I'm trying to engineer the call, I like to do what I call a soft call to action. The general principle behind the soft call to action is to approach it informally, like you would speak to a friend. When most people see legal ads on the tv, they hear the same thing:

"Call today for a free consultation."

There's nothing wrong with it, but it's impersonal. If you want to prove you're different, you have to be different. You spend time creating a piece of content, with a hook and tools to keep them engaged. Rather than closing it with the typical, "Call today for a consultation", offer up something more informal.

"If this applies to you, I'd love to talk more with you about it. Send a direct message on my channel or give me a call. Here's my number, I'd love to point you in the right direction."

Make it feel informal. Make it feel personal. Make it as simple as possible. Consultation has a sterile feel to it. Marketing is all about how you disguise the sales call. The difference between "meeting to see if I can help" and "a free consultation" is just branding. It's all about how you sell it.

These strategies can be arranged and rearranged in all the ways you communicate what you do. They can demonstrate to the market how you stand out as an attorney. I've worked with hundreds of law firms and my mission is simple. I want to help owners put more profit in their pocket and free time on their calendars. There are so many great lawyers out there who don't make enough money for how much they work. Everybody thinks lawyers are rich, except lawyers. It takes work and time and effort. At the end of all of the education, training and work, law firm owners deserve to be successful.

To arrive at a truly great law business, you have to be a really great lawyer as well as a really great entrepreneur. What I've found, after working with lawyers all over the country, is that a formulaic approach to how you market and bring people in will inevitably lead to greater profits and less demands on your schedule.

A simple framework, a simple formula, can change your life.

ALCHEMY IN ACTION:

Provide value: Impact lives upfront with your content and advertising. Build confidence in your product.

Farm ideas: Analyze techniques and practices across industries to discover new opportunities on your own.

Master the social formula: Utilize a hook, loop and call in your advertising to keep your audience engaged.

chapter 3

SETTING EXPECTATIONS
– CHARLEY

When Teddy Roosevelt Senior left the house for the day, he would turn to his wife and say, "Mind the children obey the first order." A patriarch, firm in discipline and diligent in drive, laid out a clear expectation of how the family would be directed in his absence. Leadership that would one day be passed to his son, Teddy, future President of the United States.

The greatest tenant of good leadership is setting expectations.

HIGH PERFORMERS

As a coach, I work with a lot of people who are "Personal High Performers". You'd recognize them easily if you saw them; they're driven, diligent, entrepreneurs with a talent not only to find the goal post but to discover the play they need to make to get themselves there. A topic that comes up frequently while working with these individuals is, "How do I install that higher level of performance within my firm?"

The solution to that question might seem straightforward, especially for those with a more mercenary eye towards the work, but another trait these high performers share is they are people you would be quick to categorize as good, and kind.

These two traits, which separately constitute a well-rounded person, can be at odds with one another in a professional environment.

A lot of times, high performers run into this issue where their perceived high performance rubs others the wrong way. They become anxious they'll be seen as bull-nosed, hard charging and demanding. Perhaps, in the past, they projected that image and received a negative reaction.

So how do we handle these competing interests? How do we balance the drive of high performance and the relatability and overall attractiveness of being 'good'?

BRINGING OTHERS TO YOUR LEVEL

If you are the only one living up to the expectation set for your business, you have arrived at your biggest limitation. If you are the only one expecting yourself to achieve, you alone will be able to achieve it. You'll be successful, and maybe your firm will be too. It might be success, but it's not alchemy. You can drive a firm up to, say, seven figures on the expectations you place on yourself alone, but without having higher expectations of others, there comes a hard stopping point in the practice's growth.

If we're talking about magnifying growth, constructing systems, and getting to that multimillion-dollar level, that's not going to be done on your intrinsic motivation. It needs to be done by combining intrinsically motivated individuals- people who like to achieve- with achievements for them to hit. So both their intrinsic motivators combined with you applying actual expectations, both numerically and through the culture, the values and the leadership that you establish and display within the firm.

AIM HIGH

When setting expectations don't fall into the trap of focusing on the comfort of the performer rather than your need to see something accomplished within your own parameters and timeline. For example, you're looking at a number you expect of someone; you want them to get demands sent out within 30 days of collecting all the medical bills. That is the expectation you want to set. Then, you stop and think about previous times when it was just you. Those were difficult times, it usually took you a couple of months to get them out there. 30 days is a lot to ask. You're not even sure you could do that. And all of a sudden, you're shying away and you're telling them, "I don't know, take 60 days." By falling into this trap, you've reinforced the standard you had when you were a busy solo attorney trying to do everything in the practice, and you've diluted what your firm could potentially be capable of with its present size and resources.

In setting bold, high-performance expectations, you give your team an opportunity to specialize and to be great. If you give them unlimited time to accomplish a task, the task will take an unlimited amount of time to accomplish. If you give them 30 days to accomplish, they will do everything they can to accomplish it within 30 days. In setting expectations, you give your team the opportunity to achieve the remarkable. Is it possible that they will fail? Sure, but more importantly, what if they succeed from that mindset of daring greatly? What might that do for your firm, and for them?

WHAT IF THEY FAIL?

Now it is true, there will be times when people will fall short. When you set expectations in the practice, the hardest part is the first time that you have to tell someone they didn't meet expectations. How do you have that conversation? How do you convey the importance of meeting expectations? Start with this framework:

That was the number.
We didn't hit it this time.
How do we hit it next time?

The discussion doesn't need to be punitive. The first time someone misses the mark doesn't require a severe response. Instead, consider inviting them to be a part of the solution. It can be as simple as, "Right now we're averaging 45 days to get our demands out the door. How do we get that down to 30?" You may learn there's something in the practice you don't know about. Maybe the system is clunky. Maybe the company you hired to do medical records retrieval is not living up to its end of the bargain, and we need to rebuild the process. Now you can put new systems into practice to ensure expectations will more likely be met in the future.

If you don't set expectations, you'll never have that form of discovery. You'll be in an endless loop, a hamster wheel of wondering why things aren't working better.

MAKE IT MEASURABLE

I encourage my clients to make sure their expectations and goals are measurable. You need objective metrics, and these metrics should stretch you. They should stretch your team. How do you set an objective metric, particularly if there is expressed doubt, or cynicism, from your team that it's obtainable? Step one is to figure out what your baseline is. What's your status quo number? What's the figure you and your team can coast on? Once you find it, raise that by 20%. The next step is encouragement.

"I know we can achieve this."
"I know we can work more efficiently."
"I'm going to lead you all."
"I will ask of myself the same thing I am asking of you."
"I'm going to provide the guidance.
   The encouragement.
      The coaching to get to that place."

You set expectations and you scale up. Suddenly, instead of signing ten new clients per month, you're going to sign twelve new clients per month. You have the clear, objective metric as your goal and you set the expectation to get there.

You need to get more leads, improve your intake, and streamline the process of getting people to sign. Of course, it's not enough to just say you need to do it. You must measure the outcome. Then, you grow the expected outcome. For example, imagine you look at your data and you determine that your team should get 12 new sign-ups every month. Right now, they get about 10 or 11, but they could and should get 12. So you set that as your key performance indicator. Then, as soon as you start getting twelve new sign ups, you're going to scale it to fifteen new sign ups per month. (I usually make jumps of 20-25% in increased expectation, assuming the support is provided to help the team get there.)

These are specific examples, but you can see how setting tangible, specific and forward-reaching expectations helps determine the specific steps needed to reach them.

OUTCOME EXPECTATIONS AND PROCESS EXPECTATIONS

As you begin to determine what expectations you want to set to push back that goal post, consider dividing them into two categories: outcome expectations and process expectations.

Outcome expectations are your endgame. It's the number of clients signed, or the number of matters closed. It's the picture. The objective. It's your finish line.

Process expectations are how you're going to get there. A few examples of process expectations are the number of social media posts you do in a week, the number of outbound referrals, or how many billable hours you require of your firm each week. Process expectations are the tangible metrics that help meet your outcome expectation. This is where we have to balance achieving the outcome regardless of process versus following the process and trusting the process.

Setting higher expectations is valuable. Your team wants to achieve their untapped potential and if you don't set the expectations, they will go back to their minimum selves. They'll coast. You are not building an environment for your firm to coast. You are building a place to perform, a place to realize professional goals unreachable in other places. Working in a small business that is committed to helping people, and making great money in the process, is a privilege. It is a privilege to be pushed. It is a privilege to meet expectations, to grow, to expand, to make yourself better.

BE THE CAPTAIN

If you are constructing an environment where you not only know what is possible for your team, but also push them to achieve it, some people are going to fall out. That's the other hard part about raising expectations. Some people won't make the cut. This is where we get into the discussion of the difference between being the patriarch or matriarch of your firm and being the captain. Countless work environments fall into the trap of calling themselves a family.

"We're like a family here."

"This is a family environment."

Don't fall into that trap.

Your work is not a family.

You are not running a family.

Families are messed up. All of them, even the best of ones, are reacting to emotions. We have a long, storied history of cherished memories and unavoidable wounds. We care about how people feel. You care about how your kids feel, how your spouse feels, and about how your parents feel. That's important with family.

That's not the gap your law firm is supposed to fill in someone's life. This is where you need to be the captain. You have a mission and people have to live up to that mission. And if someone can't tie the rigging- we've slipped from sports metaphors to boat metaphors- (welcome aboard.) They're endangering other members of the crew and the next time you hit port, they have to go. They have to be replaced. Because if they're not, the entire ship is on the line. When you become the captain, your job is not to cater to the emotional ups and downs. Your job is to stay on mission and keep the ship on course.

As the captain, you look to your crew as a collective, not as individuals. And the collective will only be as successful as the least performing member of that crew. And so, as the captain, you owe it to your team to have no weak links. Because-if you do-the whole thing will fall apart. You have every right, reason, and even responsibility to set higher expectations. This is one of the things I do as early as possible during consulting days with clients but I want you to hear this message now, loud and clear,

THEY DON'T TEACH YOU THIS IN LAW SCHOOL

more than anything else, that it's time for you to become the captain. The captain knows what the mission is. The captain knows what the people are supposed to do. And the captain continually reinforces when the work is good enough and when it is not.

Now, you're not going to be a pirate captain that tells people only when they're messing up. You're not going to be a mercenary. You're going to be the captain that says, "That is how it is done. You kept your course. I am proud of you for being able to accomplish that. See how the hard work pays off?" And in your firm, the hard work pays off.

So set higher expectations. Know it's okay, and know it's okay for people who do not match up with those expectations to leave.

And here's the flip side. What if other people come in and they have high expectations of what they could achieve, and you're not driven enough, as a firm, for them to achieve their goals? You're going to lose your best talent that way. They're going to walk out the door. They're going to go to a place that does expect more of them. High performers want to be in a space where more is expected of them. Learn to expect more, and you will attract them.

With the right crew in place and expectations as your compass, you'll be surprised where the journey takes you.

ALCHEMY IN ACTION:

Set higher expectations: Emphasize the importance of setting higher expectations for oneself and for others in order to achieve personal and professional growth. This involves recognizing untapped potential and pushing team members to reach their goals.

Balance outcome expectations and process expectations: Understand the difference between outcome expectations and process expectations. It is important to establish both types of expectations to ensure success.

Establish objective metrics: Use objective metrics to measure progress and performance. These metrics should be stretching for both the individual and the team, encouraging growth and improvement.

Have discussions about expectations: Engage in open and constructive discussions with team members when expectations are not met. This involves addressing the gap between the current performance and the desired outcome, identifying areas for improvement, and finding solutions together.

Replace underperforming team members: Maintain a high-performing team. If someone consistently fails to meet expectations and becomes a weak link, they may need to be replaced with someone who can fulfill the job requirements.

Recognize and reward hard work: Acknowledge and appreciate the efforts of team members. Such acknowledgement and appreciation will motivate them to continue striving for excellence.

chapter 4

CREATING A
MARKETING ECOSYSTEM
WITH KIA ARIAN

Kia Arian is CEO and founder of Zine, a marketing and brand development agency that helps attorneys, entrepreneurs, and professionals convert prospects into raving fans who trust them, stay with them, and tell others about them. From concept to design to implementation, Kia and the team at Zine specialize in high-touch, physical direct mail to present a marketing message that inspires action and generates profitable results for their clients. Kia's clients include Dan Kennedy, Ben Glass, Ben Settle and more. She has been featured on numerous podcasts and appeared on stage to teach about marketing and mindset and the entrepreneurial journey.

I'VE WORKED WITH LAWYERS for close to twenty years. They all came from a wide array of schools and backgrounds, but a common thread which seemed missing in their robust education was creativity and innovation. It's just not the nature of law, or a focus in law school. They are there to learn law, logic, analysis, and tradition. They are given lines and told to always color inside of them. Creativity and innovation can slip through the cracks. Law school prepares them to practice the law, but for managing and marketing a business? It can leave people wanting. Which is where I come in. I rarely color inside the lines, I fill the world first with color, and then add the lines when I need a shape.

My background is in computers. I had a really stellar career working with the Hubble Space Telescope before stepping into graphic design. It was an amazing place to work with amazing people. I was financially set. I was professionally set. I had my entire life laid out. But I also felt completely stifled. After ten years, I was ready to pursue a bigger vision and greater freedom for creativity. The desire for growth, adventure, and discovery is a universal part of the human journey. It comes from wanting to pursue what you feel called to do. It's also the seed that the entrepreneurial spirit is born from. I wanted the ability to create a future that aligned with my vision. I wasn't sure what exactly that looked like, but I felt compelled to find it.

Since I already had a background in computers, I decided to pursue graphic design in order to tap into the creativity I desired. I took the leap, quit my job, acquired a printshop, and got into the design and printing business. What I didn't have was a background in marketing. I fell into the trap many attorneys who start their own practice fall into. I had all the skills to provide stellar service, but no wherewithal to market it.

During a particularly slow season, we decided to market in the only way we knew how...mail a postcard. We didn't have the money to buy a list, so we looked up attorneys and accountants in our area and sent out about 100 postcards. We got about fifty returned. But one ended up in front of the right person, an attorney named Ben Glass who also taught law firm marketing, and the rest is history.

GETTING CREATIVE WITH DIRECT RESPONSE MARKETING

One of our earliest strategies that have stayed with us as we've grown is just **staying in front of people so we're there when they need us**.

No matter what your trade is, whether it's law, design, or advertising, people need to be reminded of who you are and what you do. It's not enough to master your trade or become an expert in your professional space.

You have to find your audience and stay connected with them in a meaningful way.

I found my audience in the legal world. Ben Glass was one of the essential connections who was instrumental in how I marketed my business. I used the strategies he taught law firms to clarify my marketing and grow my business. I had a retail print shop at the time, which provided a great opportunity for lawyers to utilize our services to implement what Ben was teaching.

A core attribute of creativity is the ability to take principles or ideas and adapt them to suit the work you are doing. The most successful attorney marketers I've seen have been able to adapt principles and strategies from outside the profession in really remarkable ways.

FIND YOUR WHO

Another important lesson I learned was to be willing to take a chance and focus on *who* you want to work with. You shouldn't be trying to talk to the whole world. You can't. You need to speak to the one ideal client you want to work with and cater a message that resonates with them.

Finding your who is a core principle of direct response marketing.

As I continued to grow and make shifts in my business, art and design remained part of our core work. Visual stimuli make a huge impact on how we process information and how we make decisions. It accounts for 75% of cognitive processing in our brain's primary cortical region. Most designers focus on the art and aesthetics and neglect the fact that your marketing is supposed to compel action. That's what direct response marketing is—you generate a response, preferably in your favor.

At Zine, our marketing philosophy is **seeking to engage, rather than just sell.** Don't get me wrong, we want to sell, but we believe it can be a natural part of relationship building with your prospects. Our newsletter program uses proven marketing strategies to drive conversions, referrals, and sales. Like the book written by Russell Conwell almost 100 years ago, the diamonds are at your feet. The people who already know you or have done business with you are often your best prospects. When you stay in front of them in a consistent, relevant, and engaging way, such as a print newsletter, you can convert them to raving fans who love you, stay with you, and tell others about you.

Your newsletter doesn't always need to be beautiful, or flashy. It just needs content to engage the people you are trying to reach. It needs to be personalized, and it needs to have an invitation to engage.

When you're working with any visually based media make sure:

1) It's visually engaging,
2) It's clearly aimed towards the people you're trying to reach and, most importantly...
3) There is a call to action, or invitation for them to reply.

These steps can apply to newsletters, emails, or any other type of outbound marketing.

DISSECTING YOUR MESSAGE

One of the common mistakes I see lawyers make in their marketing is focusing their message on their services, the quality of their services, the years of experience, their staff, and everything else about them. So before I start any marketing campaigns for them, we fix their message so it focuses on the problems, needs, and desired outcomes of their prospective client. This is often very different from being "aggressive and experienced" or having a big office with lots of staff.

For example, I worked with an attorney whose primary message was, "We've worked with insurance companies and know how to fight them. They have great defense lawyers. You need a lawyer to fight for you."

It's not a bad message. It's logical. It's understandable. But is it really the first thing your ideal client is thinking when they start searching for a lawyer? What if their biggest worry is their financial situation? What is their emotional state? Are they stressed and worried? Or angry and depressed? They're not thinking about the legal process, they want to trust you. Your message should present the solutions in simple terms, and the outcome they can expect. Don't just say you are compassionate, demonstrate it. **Meet people where they are and make it as easy as possible for them to connect with you.**

It's not easy to dissect your message and make it so it appeals to your ideal market. When I do it for my own marketing, it feels like I'm doing it in a vacuum. It's like you're inside the jar and trying to read the label. It's always helpful to bring somebody from the outside to give you perspective, bounce ideas off of, and help clarify your message.

For legal marketing, you can clarify your marketing message by first asking **"what is the real problem I am solving for prospective clients?"** Look at the answer from two levels.

Level One is the problem they're presented with. It's what they present to you. Someone got into an accident, or they're going through a divorce. They need legal help.

Level Two are the issues in their life arising from their level one problem. They are the underlying problems. It's financial hardship, the stress of being injured, and the disruption to their lives and peace of mind. Level two is the human element.

A good marketing message addresses both levels but focuses on Level Two.

CREATING OUTCOMES WITH COPYWRITING

"Outcome" is an important word whenever we talk about copywriting. Almost everyone has heard the idea of features versus benefits but it's easy to stumble when talking about the difference between the two.

For instance, say you're trying to sell a vacuum cleaner. You could advertise that its motor runs quietly, it's lightweight, and has the most up-to-date filtration technology. This would be an example of advertising its features. However, if you talk about how much time it will save in your daily cleaning, or how your back won't hurt carrying it around, or how much better you'll breathe, now you're selling benefits.

When you include outcome-based terminology in your copywriting, you're advertising the benefits of having extensive experience or a big staff.

When writing copy, there are two applications to consider. Copywriting for your website and copywriting for emails or other direct marketing.

SEO is an important factor for website copy. The rules for SEO seem to change constantly. So I'll share the constants which don't change over time. When someone visits the first page of your website, they should see several things. They should see what problem you solve, and they should see what life will look like after working with you. It should be simple, straightforward language that you use everywhere to reinforce it.

For all other copywriting, a method we like to use that not only saves time but is also incredibly effective is called **success stories**. An attorney takes their top cases and tells each story using a framework that makes it clear what this client's life was like before they met the attorney, and what it's like now. It is natural, outcome-based copy that tells a story and demonstrates your success.

I worked with an attorney who had great content for his social media and website. It was all about legal issues and tips and warnings about how to win your case. It was well-done, relevant content. But he was getting bored to death talking about five ways to deal with insurance companies and *three mistakes for a car accident.* He wanted to do something more interesting but didn't know what.

So we went through our process of drilling down to uncover his vision, his value proposition, his successes, and what he was passionate about. We discovered he could move away from creating legal content and have his staff create content using success stories. The stories would be collected from happy clients and repurposed across his media. Meanwhile, he could focus on creating content about personal growth and mindset—things he was passionate about.

Creating marketing content is not easy. But it's one of the most profound ways we can express our creativity as entrepreneurs. There's an immense freedom which comes from infusing your passion into your marketing and copywriting. After all, isn't that why we left our cushy jobs and embarked on a journey towards greater freedom? Use these ideas and strategies to build your practice layer by layer. Each layer by itself may seem insignificant, but when stacked together, you create a foundation that is based on what matters to you and what you have been called to do.

ALCHEMY IN ACTION:

Get creative: Adopt principles and strategies from outside of the profession and utilize them in new ways.

Find your who: Find your target audience, then seek to engage rather than sell.

Dissect your message: Meet people where they are and make it easy for them to connect with you.

chapter 5

BRANDING FOR SUCCESS
WITH TONY ALBRECHT

Tony Albrecht is a writer, social entrepreneur, and student of the creative process. Tony co-founded The Rowdy Creative and The Wilds & The Woods, and he works with people old enough to know they want a different trajectory and young and crazy enough to believe that big change is possible. His work is informed by his recovery from two afflictions, alcoholism and becoming a lawyer.

Tony uses his writing, creativity and social media savvy to help mission-driven lawyers build magnetic presences online. He is the author of The Creative Arena: Why Creativity is Key to Building Your Future.

Tony lives in a forest in Ontario, Canada, with his wife and two children, who both insist on growing up too fast.

I FINISHED LAW SCHOOL in the height of the great recession. I was living in my hometown of St. Louis and I snatched up the best offer I had straight out of law school. So I packed up my entire life, moved across the world, and took up work for a solo practitioner on the island of Guam.

I left law school with a lifetime of knowledge. Something I didn't have was perspective. When I arrived in Guam I brought, in addition to the few worldly possessions I had, an enormous ego, crippling loneliness, and a relationship with alcohol which every day was spiraling further out of my control. Within months of relocating I'd hit my rock bottom, spending the night in a Guamanian jail cell. I've written a lot about the experience but, what I'll say in summary, spending an evening behind bars gave me more perspective than law school ever did. I eventually got my head on straight and, today, my recovery is a huge part of who I am. I took my last drink on May 29, 2010, and eventually found my way back to St. Louis working on the defense side of insurance litigation. I did it for the next ten years before going into business for myself.

Today, I'm happy to say I'm in recovery from alcohol, and also from being an attorney.

DO WHAT YOU VALUE

Something I picked up along the way, which I think is invaluable for young people to begin contemplating early, is the importance of prioritizing your values and letting it inform who you want to be in the world. A side effect of the 9 to 5 culture is we tend to define ourselves by what we do. It's one of the first questions we ask when we meet someone new. "So, what do you do?" We're defined by our occupation rather than our occupation reflecting what we value.

Learning what you value, and who you are, takes time. There's an insane amount of pressure to get it right, to have a clear and linear trajectory. I fell into this thinking, certainly in my early twenties. In hindsight, I probably never should have gone to law school. It brought out the worst version of myself. Rather than embracing what I valued, and who I wanted to be, I was hiding from it. I thought being a lawyer was what would make me valuableto the world, when what I personally valued and wanted was to be a writer. I could never see it as a viable career path and so I molded myself into what I thought would make me successful.

Since then I've torched my career on two separate occasions. I put everything on pause and traveled the world. An intended one-year trip turned into four years and a dozen countries. I took my time.

I started living.

I came back with a million stories, a girlfriend (who is now my wife) and an awakened sense of who I wanted to be. I had come so far from that jail cell, and there was even further I wanted to go. By 2020 I was on track to become a partner in my firm by 2021, and I was miserable. I knew it wasn't what I wanted. I didn't want to keep doing what I'd been doing over the past fifteen years.

With the help of my wife I changed the trajectory of my life, yet again, and I never looked back. In life, we get set in these deep trenches of habit. We develop linear thinking and it puts us into a frame of mind detrimental to our growth.

This is all I am. This is the best I can do.
This is as good as it gets.

Clearly defining what you value and who you want to be doesn't just give you clarity. It gives you power. It equips you with the ability to make the hard decision that yields a better, more attuned, life.

Since leaving law school, my work ultimately has been helping law firm owners take the vision of who they are and clearly represent it to the world. When you're an entrepreneur, knowing what you value is only half the game; the other half is how you share those values to the wider world.

BRAND WHO YOU ARE.

Branding is all about who you want to be, the change you want to make, and how you choose to express those changes. It's taking the messages you share and the topics you talk about and putting it together in a coherent, cohesive way which resonates with the people you want to reach.

Branding has this connotation of being manufactured or synthetic, maybe even a bit sleazy. When it's done well, it's the opposite. Branding is about discovery. It's about digging into who you're trying to be. It's about asking questions. What are the values dictating how you go through the world? Who are you showing up for? Is it your family? Your clients? The underrepresented? The marginalized?

At the end of the day, what impact do you want to make?

There's a degree of reverse engineering which happens. Once you figure out the answer to those pretty weighty questions, you can begin to develop a strategy to broadcast those answers through your brand. The core of helping people with branding work is helping them acquire clarity in their message. Then we move on to find ways to communicate the message to effectively reach people and spread.

The platform you'll find me engaging most often is LinkedIn. I didn't go into it with the highest expectations. I had the preconceived idea, like many, that LinkedIn was for announcing job changes, sharing press releases, and blogging esoterically about the law. What I discovered was there was this incredible opportunity to get people's attention. LinkedIn's algorithm was looking for interesting, and different, things. It isn't the echo chamber other platforms become, so if you're willing to show up and say something interesting you can almost immediately punch above your weight class. You can garner a lot of attention.

There are so many people waiting to be engaged. When I think about the opportunity this presents for lawyers, I get excited. We're all familiar with how lawyers project themselves to the world. We see the billboards, the tv, and radio ads. It's all fine. It has a role. It helps with name awareness. People know what it is when they see it. LinkedIn takes it a step further though. It builds brand awareness and provides the opportunity to build connection.

There is the potential for a connection economy to share messages in more dynamic ways. It's where the real power of social media is. What you present on social media allows people to see who you are behind the ads. It introduces them to what you stand for, and what you represent, in an environment where you aren't selling anything. It's the ultimate show vs. tell.

Show up. Talk about what drives you. Talk about your personal history, your family and what you've learned along the way. Share a special project you're working on. Talk through how you're building your law firm. By sharing your perspective it doesn't just get your name out there, it builds an awareness of what's important to you. It builds interest in what you do.

Go beyond the typical announcements and updates. Tell the story behind them. Craft something compelling. Leave it all on the table.

STORYTELLING FOR THE ALGORITHM

When I started to really pay attention to LinkedIn, I took Justin Welsh's course: *The Operating System: Grow and Monetize Your LinkedIn.* It had a huge impact on me. I highly recommend it. I don't think I would be where I am had I not taken his course.

I say all of this, because the advice I'm about to share comes from what I learned from Justin.

There is this problematic focus on content. People focus on subject matter, proving expertise or sharing the event. What's often missing is the point of view. The *who* is just as important as the *what*. Your point of view is mission critical. Showing who you are while simultaneously sharing content is formulaic to social engagement.

Some easy avenues to let your individuality show through is by sharing photos, details about your family and what you're doing with your business. As you get bigger and people start to develop a level of trust in your credibility then you can get away with showing less of yourself in certain posts. The information can stand for yourself.

The same principles apply when you're chasing leads directly from clients. We need to show expertise in our subject matter, but we also need to show who we are. The world is filled with people with the same credentials and knowledge you have. There is only one of you. People inevitably bet on you because of who you are, not what you know. People aren't looking for subject matter expertise until they need it. What they're looking for is a person they can have a rapport with. They're looking for a person they can count on.

It's through repetition that you start to lodge in people's mind. You start showing up more in people's feeds and engaging with new audiences. It's going to get more of your stuff out there, not just your latest post, but things from previous weeks. Posting consistently, from a unique point of view, will make you grow.

LinkedIn has roughly 900 million users around the world, and the percentage of people posting content with any consistency is still, to my understanding, less than 5%. It's a vast, untapped environment to be seen.

There is so much noise in the world, especially across the varied social media platforms. Regardless of the platform, making a commitment to your identity and confidently saying who you are and what you value is really key.

In a time where it seems like everyone is trying to sell you something, being yourself is an act of courage. It can make you the exception to the rule, and build traction as a brand without compromising your values, or who you are.

ALCHEMY IN ACTION:

Do what you value: Let your values dictate the work you do, and how you define your career trajectory.

Build your brand: Find a social media platform you resonate with. LinkedIn has a ton of potential. Post authentically. Post honestly. Post often.

Storytelling with the algorithm: Include a personal point of view in addition to your expertise.

CLAIM $729 IN FREE RESOURCES
TO GET MORE CLIENTS, RECLAIM YOUR TIME, AND BUILD YOUR IDEAL LAW FIRM...

Add fuel to your entrepreneurial fire with our collection of guides, templates, and how-to information, guaranteed to help you:

- Generate high-quality, pre-sold leads for your law firm (so you can stop worrying about whether or not the phone is going to ring this week)

- Improve your leadership skills through superior communication techniques (which translate just as well to communication with a spouse or partner)

- Take back control of your marketing (including how to communicate with and hold your vendors accountable)

- Develop a stronger brand message (with a big, bold promise)

- Master your core financial numbers (so your firm runs like a well-oiled, profit-generating machine instead of a "what's happened lately" patchwork of decisions)

- And more!

This package of resources is exclusively for readers of this book, and to claim yours, just go to:

WWW.LAWFIRMALCHEMY.COM/VOLUME1

Go right now to get your hands on these free gifts for you!

chapter 6

BECOMING THE CAPTAIN OF YOUR SHIP
– CHARLEY

I MENTIONED, towards the end of my last chapter, "you have to become the captain of your own ship." I want to take a few pages to unpack this perspective shift. It's one of the most dynamic ways I've learned to shift how you operate your business, so batten down the hatches while I pass it along.

I really love sharing what I've learned. I love distilling the things I pick up inside the business, all of the coaching calls, and all the years. I like putting into words the ideas percolating inside my head and giving them the opportunity to be heard, especially when they can help other people's journey and help them grow.

A lot of the firm owners I work with are in the mid-to-upper six figures, and well on their way to adding another digit onto the end. There's a transition that's endemic to this particular stage. A transition that's essential to raising the bar and meeting the new challenges that arise head on. More than anything else it's a change of perspective, leaving behind the 'patriarch or matriarch' stage and becoming the **captain of the ship**.

STARTING THE JOURNEY

This new journey in leadership is not an easy one. It's less about deciding where to allocate your resources and much more about determining and pursuing your vision relentlessly. It's about how you set up your team and your firm for success... without you putting in the normal daily grind. I understand the desire to have your law firm "feel like a family." There's a sentimentality about it – a warmth and comfort akin to someone's favorite sitcom. Everyone chips in and helps out. Sure, mom and dad are at the top of the food chain, but no one is really above the other. Those days are about to end. It's time for someone to chart the course and hold the crew accountable. It's time to be the captain.

When you have four to six employees, it's natural and even helpful to have a deeper relationship with them. It's okay to know them more, to wrap your arms around the whole place as the head of the family.

It's fundamentally different when you move from the head of the family to captain of the ship. If you try to keep that sense of family when you grow to twenty employees it can start to cause problems.

As you start to grow you have to change the way you view your role in leadership. I will say again, it's hard.

One of the things I want to emphasize here is this transition, deliberately putting emotional distance between you and your staff doesn't make you a bad person. You will actually help your team in the end. You are going to help them perform at a higher level.

As the head of the family, there is an implication that you exist to provide for your family. Why I think this shift in role is so effective is how it alters this frame of mind. As the Captain of the ship, you exist to fulfill a mission. Your goal is to safely get the ship to its destination. Your crew exists to help you get there. If there are crew members who cannot keep up, they put the lives of the other people on the boat at risk. If there is a crew member who requires way more resources than someone else, they are going to be a drain on morale. They're going to cost time, resources, and progress, none of which help the mission.

You see where this is going. As the captain, you have to make decisions for the good of the whole crew. It means making tough decisions. Sometimes, it means letting people go. I'm not implying you need to acquire a certain degree of ruthlessness. Becoming the captain requires the same amount of compassion and care, you're just caring in a different way.

CARING AS THE CAPTAIN

As the head of the family, you develop a relationship with every individual who is under you. You care about them on a personal level. Your transition point, when you become the captain, is to care about the team. That's your transition point.

In caring about the team, you naturally have to care about individuals, but you can't bend the entire crew to address the needs of one person.

You have to begin to cultivate a culture of performance. Every member of your team needs to have a stake in the mission. They need to have a clear, defined, and measurable role for how to see the mission through successfully. They need to be motivated to perform at their highest, as well as their best. The end goal becomes the betterment of everyone. Things like professional goals, financial gain, and emotional support become core values spread across an entire team and you have a culture that reflects it.

Setting expectations also becomes streamlined. Your team becomes accustomed to expectations because you set them regularly. Your expectations become proactive rather than reactionary because, if your team is functioning properly, you never have to single out any one person.

THE CAPTAIN'S ROLE

This whole journey is an adventure. Treat it that way. You are going to wander into unfamiliar territory and need to learn new skills. As you build your law firm, never lose sight of the growth you need from yourself to lead your whole firm to the best version of itself.

You're going into new territory. A multi-million-dollar firm has new marketing needs, management demands and financial structures that need to be in place. Your job as captain is to reduce the fog of war around your crew, grab your compass and navigate strongly as your team makes decisions. Your job is to keep the ship on course, which means certain things on the ship simply aren't going to be a priority. Sure you can roll up your sleeves and trim the sails, but when dozens of other people can do it and you're the only one who can chart the course, it's clear where your priority needs to be. The captain should not be responsible for the minutiae in a well-run, or a well-captained, law firm.

Nautical terms aside, manual labor isn't your job anymore. It's not even your job to oversee the manual labor. It needs to be in the capable hands of someone else. Your job is to look at the big picture.

ASSEMBLING YOUR CREW

There's a phrase I'm borrowing from a few other coaches in the world of professional development. When you're trying to tackle a big problem, ask yourself, "**Who, not how?**"

It's been mentioned a few times in the book already, but I feel like it's perfectly suited for our metaphor of ship's captain and crew.

I'm gonna turn the phrase on its head. Being the captain means being the 'Who' to someone else. It's about you creating a place where you help others fulfill their dreams, as they are helping you fulfill your bigger dream. Is your mission big enough to have crew members lining up to come on board? Is your firm first-rate enough for a new hire to accept the high expectations you'll set as captain?

Let's say you own a firm and you're acquiring a dozen clients every single month. You walk out and say to your team,

"You know what, I want you to sign 50 clients every single month."

You set the expectation, but you don't spend a single dollar on marketing. You don't learn about intake or bring on a trainer. You don't improve the way you monitor finances. You're trying to acquire fifty clients a day with a system still built for acquiring one. The math won't math.

Assembling the right crew also means equipping them with the resources they need to thrive. Leave port with a ship well-stocked with food and provisions. Set your team up for success. You're asking a lot of them, which means much must be given in return. **Your team will only be as successful as you make them. You will only be as successful as your team.**

I know so many firm owners who are actively pursuing this transition right now. It starts as a mental transition. There are resources, there are changing strategies, but it begins with an outlook shift.

Maybe the analogy of shifting from the head of the family to the captain doesn't resonate but, what it really comes down to, is a change of mind. There comes a point when leveling up means taking a less hands-on role in the day-to-day and casting your eyes on your business. It's this shift that will turn your business into your legacy. Into your empire.

However you frame it, be bold in this new chapter of your firm. Once you're out, on those wider waters, you have the chance to change a lot of lives.

Anchors away....

ALCHEMY IN ACTION:

Start the journey: Adjust your mindset away from being the head of a family, to becoming the captain of a ship.

Adjust how you care: Care for the culture as a whole, rather than on an individual basis.

Assemble your crew: Focus on the "Who?" rather than the "How?"

chapter 7

EMPATHETIC ENTREPRENEURSHIP
WITH LEN SPADA

Leonard Spada is the founder of Spada Law Group LLC. Upon graduating from Boston College Law School in 1991, Len accepted a prestigious one-year appointment as a Judicial Law Clerk for the justices of the Massachusetts Superior Court. It was during this time that Len worked closely with the Judges of the Superior Court assisting them in deciding matters that came before the court in both civil and criminal trials. The clerkship was a valuable opportunity for Len to learn the practice of law from some of the finest legal minds in Massachusetts.

Len has been named a Massachusetts Super Lawyer as published in Boston Magazine for 10 consecutive years (2013-2022) in the area of Personal Injury Law. Super Lawyer rates lawyers across the country and recognizes no more than the top 5 percent of lawyers in each state. Attorneys are selected using a patented rigorous, multiphase process that includes independent research, peer nominations, and peer evaluations. Len also has a "Superb" rating of "10" on Avvo.com, which rates attorneys *based in part on public data collected on each attorney. In 2021 Len was selected and listed in Boston Magazine's inaugural list of the Best Lawyers in the region. Len is a proud member of the Massachusetts Academy of Trial Attorneys. Len is also a frequent faculty member at Massachusetts Continuing Legal Education, where he teaches young lawyers various litigation skills, including taking depositions. Len is also the author of What You Need To Know About Your Massachusetts Car Accident Case: Before You Make Any Legal Decisions*

Len's expertise is vital for anyone looking to empower and find the next layer of leaders, across generations, within your practice.

LAW SCHOOL CHANGES the way you think. It's subtle, happening on nearly a subconscious level, but it happens. Your mind is trained to be annoyingly analytical. It's vital in the courtroom, and in practice. You're able to analyze the situation in front of you, spot issues and solve problems. Where it becomes annoying is when you punch out at the end of the day and leave it in the office.

Suddenly, you're thrust into a world where the majority of people don't think like you. Not everyone is looking for their problems to be solved. The analytical mind of an attorney can baffle, and even frustrate, the people closest to you. There are a minority of circumstances and settings where you need to turn down the volume of the lawyer's brain.

Sometimes, empathy is needed more than analysis.

Sometimes, before you leap to solve everyone's problem it's better to make sure you hear them.

LISTEN AND LEARN

The ability to sit and really listen to someone is a superpower. Too often in meetings or personal conversations I'm talking to someone and, while I'm in the middle of talking, I can tell they're already formulating a response in their head. They're just biding their time until it's their turn to talk again. You can just see it in their eyes. They're not listening, they're just waiting to respond.

If you can get good at listening, people are naturally more drawn to you. They open up to you more. They engage with you more. They're more comfortable. It's not an easy skill, but if you're early enough in your career to work at it, the return on investment is enormous. It's something I certainly could have stood to learn earlier, and a piece of advice I'd definitely love to give to my younger self.

Try to be more aware of what people are saying to you, especially when what they are giving you is advice. When somebody gives you a piece of critical advice, take some time to sit with it. Don't dismiss it outright, ponder it. It might be their bias. It might be a quirk on their end. It might also be just the window into your shortcomings you need to reach the next level. Looking back, I never gave the possibility of somebody else being right enough of a chance.

If you take the time to think about it, you will over time accelerate the pace with which you become a better person. You will become a better listener, a better thinker, and overall you'll become less annoying. For an attorney in a world of non-attorneys, I think that's a pretty damn good aspiration. As a trained lawyer, you can get to the point where your training has made you difficult in some social settings. You're perfectly suited for court, perfect for a deposition, and not-so-perfect for the dinner party. No memorable Thanksgiving begins with opening remarks. Well, maybe a memorable one does but certainly not a good one…

It's a good reminder for every lawyer who's looking to elevate past the game of being a lawyer and begin the entrepreneurship journey.

Think like a Lawyer. Listen like a friend.

THE ENTREPRENEURIAL JOURNEY

These days I'm on the upward arc of a much bigger journey. At this point in my life, I'm at an age when the topic of retirement comes up a lot. People ask if I'm thinking of slowing down. It used to really eat at me. Society has dictated that once you reach a certain age, it's time to start thinking about the pasture. I'm supposed to join the other elders and walk off into the sunset, never to be seen again.

I didn't want to. I had built my business. I learned more about marketing. I had all these skills necessary to grow my firm. I stopped thinking in the binary of *to retire* or *not to retire,* and instead asked *What do I want from life? What is my purpose?*

And I had no idea. It was such a sad revelation. It took a lot of thinking and self-searching, but eventually I found it. When I did, it totally energized me. I broke through all of those doubts about retirement with a velocity and drive I never had before. I wanted to grow my firm. I wanted to help people. There would be no horizon of retirement to walk towards.

Honestly, I never even liked the word retirement. Retirement, to me, sounds like retreat. It's an action you take when you want to get away from something you hate doing. I've always loved what I do. Why would I run from it?

I love practicing law. I love building a law firm made in the image of what I want it to be. Something aligned with my vision. Having made the decision to grow, I feel more energized in my late fifties than I ever did in my thirties, or even my twenties. If you ever find yourself in doubt about what direction to go, find where the energy is and barrel towards it. Do what energizes you.

I wake up in the morning and I'm dying to go to work. I feel deep gratitude for it. I know so many people who lie awake on Sunday night filled with dread, because they have to go to work in the morning. It's an awful mindset to have, and I feel so genuinely grateful it doesn't apply to me. Sunday comes and I get excited. I get my notepad out. I plan my workweek. I still have bad days, and they can be really daunting. Owning your firm means everything gets magnified. The bad hits you harder but the good? The good eclipses the bad a thousandfold.

No matter what I'm going through, good or bad, it's exciting as hell. I feel like it's important to highlight that I'm speaking only about my journey. I arrived here after a lot of seasons prioritizing other things. I raised my children, coached their teams, and picked them up from school. If it's not the season to pour all of your energy into growing your firm, don't get discouraged. The time will come. It was a long road to get to where I am. I've arrived at a place, now, where I can let the core of what motivates me drive my business. If you aren't there yet, you can at the very least begin thinking about your core. What drives you? What impact do you want to have on the world? What gets you out of bed in the morning?

FIND YOUR CORE

I grew up in the city. When I was a child, I grew up in a predominantly Italian immigrant neighborhood. My family was from Italy. My neighbors were from Italy. Their neighbors were from Italy.

It was gritty.

It was urban.

It was loving and it was close.

We all lived in one, triple decker, apartment building. One floor for my grandparents, another for my aunt and uncle, and one for my family. It's very similar to how many Hispanic families choose to live: large extended families in close proximity to one another. As a child, I saw what it meant to be an immigrant in America. There were distinct challenges caused by language and caused by prejudice. I was drawn to feel compassion for people who were new to this country and didn't speak the language. I developed a drive to fight for the underdog, and it carried me in my legal career.

As a prosecutor in Boston, I advocated for victims of crimes. I was vested with this "fight for the little guy" mentality. I hated bullies. I got scrappy. I practice law a mile from where I grew up. A lot of those neighborhoods have shifted in their demographics. It's all Latinos and Hispanics, but I still see so many of the qualities and struggles I grew up with among

Italian immigrant communities. Advocating for them comes naturally to me. While I'm not Hispanic, my entire staff is. We've developed a reputation in the community for standing by Latino immigrants in their fight for representation.

We do personal injury work exclusively, and we use it as a vehicle to help them. These people come to this country. The language is different. They have all types of challenges. We exist to put them on a level playing field with large insurance companies. We're actively, and empathetically, giving them the home court advantage they wouldn't otherwise have. It electrifies me. I love it.

The incredible thing is we're purpose driven and we're thriving. We're growing. We're hiring. While other people my age are scaling down, or handing over the reins, we're ratcheting up. It's exciting from a business point of view. It's exhilarating from a personal point of view. I feel like I am honoring who I am, and where I came from, and my business is thriving while I do it. Money comes with it. We're doing financially well, but it's a byproduct. It's not what gets me up in the morning. It's a combination for a really fulfilling life.

If you can manage your business where you're honoring both your purpose and your growth, everything else falls into place. If you're striving only for a dollar, things get lost in translation. You never fulfill your full potential.

EMPATHETIC ENTREPRENEURSHIP

My core isn't just outward facing, into the community, it's also inward with how I relate to my staff. I believe in paying them well, investing in them. It feels good, as a law firm owner, to know the people you have been working with feel appreciated and well-compensated. It's rewarding to see them buy their first home or put their kids through school. You feel a part of something bigger than yourself. It's rewarding.

As a father, I had the privilege of watching my children grow into incredible people. As an entrepreneur, I get to see these young staff members grow into young professionals. I get to pay them like professionals. I get a huge kick out of it.

I've gotten better and better over the years at trusting my staff. We all read things on social media about these younger generations. They're lazy. They're entitled. They're snowflakes. I'm sure you've heard them all. It really irks me. My children don't reflect the stereotype and I don't see any evidence of it in my staff. I find hardworking, passionate, and committed young people. I see people my age groaning about lazy, young people not wanting to work. I'm sure the previous generation said the same about me as we were coming up. In my experience, it's not the responsibility of the older generation to just write them off. It's our privilege to lift them up and empower them.

There is talent out there and something unique about the younger generation; they are focused on vision. They are less inclined to work for someone solely because of the money. They want mission. They want values. They want to make a difference. If you have young people on your staff, practice some of the advice I would give to my younger self, take some time to listen to them. Find out what sets them on fire. See where your values align. See how they want to change the world.

STEPPING OUT INTO OTHER COMMUNITIES

For any firm looking to reach new communities, there are several things to ask yourself. First, look in the mirror and ask yourself,

> *"Do I feel committed to helping the community*
> *for a reason other than just getting a revenue stream*
> *from that community?"*

It's okay for money to factor into it. Everyone needs money. A business needs revenue. It's not an evil thing, so don't shy away from it. However, there needs to be an underlying commitment outside of just financial gain. It can just be a desire to help an underserved community. Everyone deserves good legal representation. Those communities don't always get it because of their cultural differences.

If you have a reason to serve that community, in addition to a financial one, the next step is to show the community you have a desire to attract them as a client. They may not immediately understand why. They don't have a lot of attorney outreach from non-Spanish speaking attorneys. If you don't have a bilingual staff member, I highly recommend hiring one. It might be a challenge if you don't have language as a resource. If you can't bring someone on full-time, a virtual assistant is a great alternative. I might add, virtual assistants are all the rage right now. We use them as well. It gives you the option to hire someone from another country who speaks perfect English but can also communicate in whatever language you need. You can put them on your phone system with a VoiceOver and no one knows they're not in your office.

We have some clients come in and ask, "Where's Jose?" And they have no idea Jose is in Honduras. They fostered the same relationship with him as they have with us, and neither of us have ever met him in person.

Once you have someone bilingual in your office as a resource, get all of your documents translated. Spend the money to do it. Have everything you cover available in Spanish. Make sure people who come in feel like they belong, like they are in the right place.

These are just the first steps, enough to get you started on the journey. This community is growing. They are here to stay. If you're a young lawyer, I highly recommend growing with it instead of against it. Make the commitment now to market to the Hispanic community.

It's not a luxury, but a necessity, to grow. Make the change incrementally. I invite anybody that's interested in marketing to the Latino community to reach out to me. I'm easy to get a hold of. I mean it, if you're committed to helping that community, please reach out. Wherever you may be, if there is a community that needs help, please let me help.

I am a huge believer in the Japanese philosophy of Kaizen. It's based on making small, incremental changes towards a goal. We're naturally resistant to big change. It's a survival mechanism. It's uncomfortable to leave our comfort zone. I think it's why, across generations, there is a natural prejudice when communities begin to grow and change.

Whether you're looking to help these communities, or grow your firm, find the small steps first and, bit by bit, make the world better.

ALCHEMY IN ACTION:

Listen and learn: Develop the superpower of listening.

Find your core: Discover what fuels your passion and interests and ensure there it is at the forefront of the work you do.

Stepping into other communities: Find reasons, in addition to revenue, to step into new communities.

chapter 8

GREAT BEGETS GREAT
WITH TIM SEMELROTH

Tim Semelroth is a member of the Million Dollar Advocates Forum, the International Society of Barristers, and the American Board of Trial Advocates. He has been listed in the Great Plains Super Lawyers since 2014. Prior to practicing, Tim clerked for the Honorable John Jarvey, Chief Magistrate Judge, US District Court for the Northern District of Iowa from 1997-1998.

He served as President of the Iowa Association for Justice, 2008-2009 and has been a Master of the American Inns of Court since 2015. Tim lectures extensively for local and national organizations including AAJ, ABA and numerous Iowa associations.

ONE OF THE SMARTEST THINGS that anybody's told me about the practice of law is this:

Great cases make Great lawyers.

If you aspire to be great, you have to put yourself in situations to compel greatness. You need great cases. It can look like hooking your wagon to a mentor with a reputation for attracting great cases. It can look like making a commitment to marketing to bring great cases to you. Skill or talent has little to do with it. You can be the best technician in the world. You can be absolutely fantastic at opening statements. You can be eloquent, diligent, and precise. However, you won't be appreciated as great, financially or by reputation, if you're not working on great cases.

I grew up the oldest of five kids. My father worked in a factory. My mom was a schoolteacher. I was a kid in desperate need of a mentor. I looked for them everywhere in my life, whether it was on my high school wrestling team or college as I began looking towards a career in law. I felt in my gut that my road to greatness was tied to finding a great mentor. I found my way into a judicial clerkship straight out of law school and spent a lot of time getting to know different judges in my native state of Iowa.

Finding the right mentor became the central theme of my professional journey. I chose opportunities to work side by side with lawyers whom I admired over money, or prestige, because I wanted to learn from them. I wanted their help to become a great lawyer. Once I took a leadership role as an owner in my firm, it translated to becoming the best marketer I could be. I didn't want to find great cases because they were referred to me. I wanted the great cases to be able to find me.

FOLLOW THE BASICS

Owning my own firm and a passion for learning ultimately pointed me in the direction of discovering all the different ways I could market our firm and bring cases in.

The biggest lesson I've learned is you can't fail if you **follow the basics** and keep them implemented no matter what level your firm is sitting. A lot of firms, when they reach six figures and upwards, start slowing down with marketing. Marketing isn't just about bringing the great cases to you. It's also about showing the world who you are as a firm. Our systems aren't complicated, but they've gotten us where we want to be and keep us delivering the quality service we want to be known for.

One basic tenant I live by is **tending to your herd.** Identify the people who you know and respect as lawyers and make sure you're at the top of their minds for case referrals. Send out a monthly newsletter with updates about your firm but also, make it personal. Take the time to send holiday cards, birthday cards, and congratulations when the occasion warrants.

The Maven's list is a professional tool we've developed and utilized over the years. Our list is composed of people who have referred cases we've accepted on more than one occasion, people who are a consistent source of referrals. Four times a year they get a gift from us. Sometimes it's a book, other times it's food. One year we sent everyone on our list a roadside assistance kit. It doesn't need to be grand, just something to make your "herd" feel valued. They're taking the time to think of us, so we want to make sure they know we're thinking of them as well.

It's a lot easier to market to people who already know that you're good at your job. When you're good at your job, growth is inevitable. This leads me to another basic tenant every firm owner will reconcile with in the course of their journey. There will come a point where you won't be able to handle the entire workload yourself, despite the feeling of infallibility which often comes from being a practicing attorney. The only way to continue to keep up with the basics as you grow is to **hire people you trust.** Find a marketing director who understands, and shares, your vision. Find a person who can design a newsletter better than you. Bring on the person who will send the holiday card out on time. If great lawyers are made by great cases, great owners are made by great employees. Get all of those things out of your way so you can continue to try great cases.

Utilize the people, and technology, around you to continue to expand your business. We live in an age of huge innovation. Everyday new software and tech is released, streamlining the way we approach our businesses and providing opportunities to accelerate our growth. Throughout my career, I've remained on the cutting edge of marketing and technology within the legal field without compromising the ethics framing the core of my practice.

The two things aren't antithetical to one another. There's a path to synergies between the two.

MERGING MARKETING AND TECHNOLOGY

I really love shiny objects.

I'm enamored with the idea that there is a new tool out there which can make me a better lawyer, and may make us better. I'm constantly on the lookout for it. Anytime I find system breakdowns in my practice, or professional shortcomings, I look for a way technology can supplement. It's important to note technology can't replace diligence, but it can certainly enhance and supplement certain areas where your energy could serve to be spared.

I have a great example of this. I was absolutely abysmal at managing my email inbox. A friend of mine recommended a service where a virtual assistant curates your inbox, and it was a game changer. It's been huge for me, professionally.

Technology can also provide avenues to ensure that free information you provide remains relevant and accessible. I used to give a large amount of free information away to people on DVD, which at this point in the 21st century has more or less become obsolete. Staying up to date on what platforms are available to you allows you not only to continue present practices, but also to level them up. I found an online course platform which allowed me to continue to give free information but do it with an extended reach to bring people back to my firm.

It's being open to new tools. It's all about embracing change, which can be hard at times. I usually have to hear about a new service or technology two or three times in different settings. It takes a degree of public confidence from people I respect. Once I do, it's exciting to dive in and figure out how to use this new tool. I teach myself the basics, but depending on the level it will come into play I'll often recruit someone on my team to be the resident expert.

Warren Buffet says, "never invest in anything you don't understand." When it comes to new systems for your firm, take the time to understand it and, most importantly, understand the role it can play in benefiting your firm.

THE ENGINE FOR SUCCESS

I don't think my journey to becoming a law firm owner is necessarily unique, or special. I imagine a lot of owners might have a story like mine. I share the story so you can glean what you can from it and see how the career progression from lawyer to firm owner can be divided into chapters.

The two guys who founded my firm, prior to me taking it over, were both contemporaries. Over ten years they developed a boutique practice primarily known for medical malpractice cases. I was the first attorney they hired to help with the caseload. For the first decade I was there I did whatever they needed me to do. I did everything from writing, research, cases and depositions. I didn't have my hand on any of the business pieces at all. I spent almost ten years focusing solely on the practice of law. When one of the founders became a judge, I made partner almost by default. The workload was immense. It was way too much for two lawyers with their eyes on running the business as well. The process sort of repeated itself. Just like they recruited me to be a lawyer, we went out and brought another lawyer on. We hired Presley, who had an expertise in nursing home litigation, and we opened our practice to an entirely new avenue for cases. We leveled up.

I realized we didn't have to be confined to medical malpractice. We can be deliberate and add new practice areas. Eventually, we stepped into workers compensation, and social security disability. We went from a medical malpractice firm to an injury and disability firm. It's how we described ourselves. Eventually, Presley would make partner and wed be asked to take over as owners of the firm. We work in all corners of the state of Iowa.

We began to gain a reputation for what we did. Lawyers with certain focuses would see us dipping our toe in an area and offer to sell us their practices. People became aware of our brand, the quality we were striving for, and they provided us with opportunities.

Looking back, the growth was natural. We'd find a lawyer specializing in something we didn't do and we brought them on board. We could support them because we have a great marketing system, a great staff, and we've built an infrastructure which allows people to come to us.

There are three chapters to growing with your firm. **Learn your practice well. Learn business well. Be open to the opportunity to grow.**

Focus on the mindset of being open to available opportunities. It's easy to fall into the trap of saying, "Hey, this is working great. This is enough." Remaining open provides the chance to scale up, to discover something even greater. If it makes sense from a business standpoint, pursue it.

Build the machine to feed you great cases. Allow the great cases to make you great. Set up the engine for your success.

THE BIG LESSON

As you grow, you're going to need great people. People say you should never go to the grocery store hungry. In the same spirit, you shouldn't go looking to hire when you desperately need a position filled.

I've made my share of bad hires, and I'll tell you I can trace it to two things. Number one is I was hungry. I was desperate for help, I found someone and immediately put too much on them. It's a huge mistake to make. The second mistake, along the same vein, is hiring people for experience and not attitude.

On paper it seems great. You're able to bring someone on who can hit the ground running. However, what they think is busy is not necessarily what you think is busy. What they think is right doesn't necessarily match with what you say is right.

Part of staying in a growth mentality is searching for people before you need to fill a role. Always be hiring, in one way or another. Give yourself permission to post an ad without necessarily having to fill it if the right candidate doesn't walk through your door.

It's a huge philosophy to adopt. It's huge for what it does for your practice. It gives you the freedom, if you find an incredible candidate, to match the role to the person rather than the other way around.

It's game-changing for your firm in the long run.

The ways and means you can bring people on, and they can serve your firm, are so varied. This might be a charged statement, but the pandemic did so many wonderful things for how we operate in the workplace.

The pandemic forced us to learn how to be good at practicing remotely. It forced us to adopt so many different technologies at once. Whether it was moving to a cloud-based case management system, learning how to use Zoom effectively, or developing a meeting schedule different from walking down the hall and talking to somebody, the pandemic primed the pump for growth. It encouraged us to think beyond Cedar Rapids.

It also makes you more flexible in terms of how you accommodate what people want in their jobs. The possibilities for remote work, hybrid, and pastime provide greater flexibility and expand the talent pool. There are ways to measure and monitor what staff do, no matter where they are. It also means, no matter where the members of my team I value choose to go, there is a place for them with my firm through the possibility of remote work.

Investing in that infrastructure really does help you in the talent acquisition stage and the talent retention stage. You can be the kind of job people want to get and want to keep.

AN IDEA TO AN INDUSTRY

A huge reason I'm a lawyer today is a program called **mock trial.** I participated all through middle school to college and it's what drew me to law school. After law school, I got involved coaching at the middle and high school levels. For the past 25 years I've served as a coach, getting the next generation excited and enthusiastic about the practice of Law.

All three of my kids have been involved, but when my son Joe was in high school, he had an experience which would shape the trajectory of his life. He went up against a team who clearly hadn't been coached by someone with a knowledge of practicing law. They won, and it was an entirely unsatisfactory victory.

We talked about it and got an idea. He created Mock Trial 101. He bought the domain and everything. He launched an online course platform with over five hundred lessons . In just a short amount of time, he's influenced hundreds of students who have benefited from the lessons.

He did it. He was successful, but it didn't stop there. He was approached to make something similar for the Commonwealth of Virginia. He did, and he was approached by a lawyer in Kentucky to do the same. Washington. New York. His idea was suddenly in demand, everywhere.

He had one caveat for making it. It had to remain a free resource for students. I'm not sure, as of writing this, where it will go. He's applying to colleges presently and I know the experience will be something which benefits him. What stands out, to me, from Joe's story is the contagious power of an idea.

Joe had an experience which showed him a need. From the need came an idea. The idea yielded action. Action inspired involvement. Greatness, from just a few simple steps.

I said at the beginning of the chapter great lawyers are made by great cases. In the modern world, I think we can mold the maxim to accommodate the infinite avenues leading to success. Great people are made by great ideas. Ideas are just the spark, though. It's the small, systematic steps taken after which solidify someone's potential and transforms it into greatness.

ALCHEMY IN ACTION:

Follow the basics: Follow proven techniques at every stage of your firm's growth.

Embrace new technology: Incorporate new technology to streamline the work, and allow you to excel.

The engine for success: Learn your practice well. Learn the business well. Be open to the opportunity to grow.

chapter 9

LESSONS FROM A FEEDBACK LOOP – CHARLEY

I'M ALWAYS THINKING: what is the most evergreen piece of lead generation that I can install within the business. Really, it is an objective for everyone's business, right? Building your list. You secure your clients of tomorrow by keeping in touch with your clients of today.

One effective technique I've made use of is a **feedback loop**. A feedback loop is the process of soliciting information from people, analyzing the information, and responding to the information. It can come in the form of surveys, polls, or direct customer contact.

In this instance, it came in the form of two pieces of lead bait sent out to my email list. The first was about **creating the habits of high performing, seven figure law firm owners.**

The second was **the five highest returns on investment marketing strategies for law firms**.

I predicted the idea of "better return on investment for your marketing" would be the winning product. It's a known desire no matter what size of firm. Firm owners understandably want to get a better return on their marketing dollars whether it's a six-, seven-, or eight-figure firm.

I had everyone up and down the revenue ladder respond. For the people on my list who weren't my clients (note the specific qualifier), there was a 75/25 split in favor of my marketing report. (As a side note, I wish it wasn't actually 75/25, because that number sounds too clean to be real. But it was.)

What I found really interesting was that for my existing clients, the response for the habits report was equal to the marketing one. It was literally right down the middle - a perfect 50/50. This struck me as significant. In marketing, you have to balance the desire to go broad (casting a wide net) versus narrowing the message to your ideal client (fishing with specific bait). From my feedback loop, I learned that half of my current clients would rather know about habits while the other half wants high ROI on marketing strategies. What incredible information to have as a marketer!

The Feedback Loop was a double win. In this instance, the marketing report will grow my list faster, while the habits report can then be offered to start sorting out who on my list is more likely to become a client.

This **feedback** has a material effect on how I market even today.

DON'T JUST GET CALLS, GET THE RIGHT CALLS.

The fruits of effective marketing aren't just getting a bunch of downloads of a report. **It's not about getting a bunch of phone calls. It's about getting the right phone calls.** It's about getting the right downloads, the right form fills, and the right entries in your live chat. Using Feedback loops, testing splits, are an effective piece of lead generation. It allows you to operate with more information, and with the new information comes confidence.

I developed this piece the same way I would have with a client. I identified the feedback I didn't have from my clients yet and figured out a robust mechanism to push me in the direction of where my gaps were. With anything like this, it's best to **start small.** Build out a basic report, or a checklist, because first you want to determine how attractive the topic is before you invest more time into it.

Once you have the feedback loop established, you can go deeper right away. You can create something a bit more complex, and in depth, than a basic checklist.

I mention checklists because they're a great default for an offer. Also, they're fast to set up! You can have an offer constructed in a matter of a couple hours if you go the checklist route.

Once you have the checklist up and running, you can start expanding the offer and making it more robust. Set up guidelines and structure around the ideas you shared. Tell them what questions they should ask when hiring a lawyer and what to look for during an initial consultation. Identify case results and testimonials. **Don't just claim your expertise, show your expertise.**

AUTHORITY PIECE

A great way to make it an invitation is with a solid authority piece. Every firm can benefit from having some type of authority piece outside of the "call to action" to reach out to the firm. It can be a simple download, an offer, or a booklet. It's a gesture of goodwill, and it creates an opportunity to follow up with people. Create something motivating people to follow up.

A lot of my coaching clients need help immediately. They need help acquiring more clients, the right way, and getting systems in place to support their growth. The difference between good client acquisition and good marketing is narrow. If good marketing is about getting the right calls, good client acquisition is about getting the right clients. They have the same end objective.

It's all about bringing people to you who are the right fit for your service. It's how you build a well-known, and well established, brand. It's how you become known for what you do, and the outcomes you generate. It's the road to a long lasting, sustainable brand.

It begins by looking at this feedback loop you create in the marketplace and asking questions. What are these subsets of data and how can they inform the bigger picture?

In my case, if I had found out that all of my existing clients wanted the high-power habits report, I would have made the high power habits report my primary lead generation device.

The marketing piece may have the numbers, but the habits piece has my market. My ideal client wants habits.

If you are creating an offer for your firm beyond a free consult, this is a great way to start thinking about it. It's how you get away from topics you really want to talk about and learn what the client wants to talk about. It's the gateway to the space you can curate and create for your market.

A real leader is constantly thinking about what the people need. What are they asking for? If I can get them in the room, then I can talk to them about bigger, bolder ideas. Start by addressing their needs first and then forging forward together.

ALCHEMY IN ACTION:

The biggest RoI: Strive to aim wide *and* aim true

Start small: Don't just get calls. Get the right calls.

chapter 10

PROTECTING PEOPLE IN A SHIFTING WORLD
WITH GREG DUPONT

Greg DuPont is a Columbus-based entrepreneur with a passion for helping others achieve financial success and legal clarity. As an attorney and financial advisor, he's mentored and coached fellow professionals, working to make a positive impact on countless families.

Greg is on a mission, "The March to a Million," aiming to positively impact one million US families by 2030.

Greg develops a personal relationship with his clients and secures wealth using proven strategies to eliminate risk, reduce lifetime tax costs, and generate more disposable income. Greg helps attorneys, professionals, and small business owners to make sure that their money supports their life and the way they want to live it.

HUMILITY IS UNDERRATED. Humility, in the world of law firms and lawyers, is often in short supply.

There are many humbling experiences throughout law school, not the least of which for me was receiving a D my first semester in property law. It certainly threw off my career trajectory, but it did a lot to teach me humility.

There's a certain level of intellectual capacity that makes one gravitate towards Law School. There's a certain level of drive that compels someone to go through that experience, and, for many, there's a certain level of financial expectation that comes with going out the other side. It's a perfect stew of anti-humility.

After conquering the dragon of law school, many of us are a little fuller of ourselves than we have a right to be. We think we have all the answers, the brains, the tenacity to go out and take over the world. In reality, at that point in our life, we have so much more growing to do. There are plenty of lawyers who leave law school confidently, but I know a lot of great ones who left humbled.

When I started my practice, I wanted to go to law school to be a joint JD-MBA. I always wanted to be a business guy. I went to law school to build my entrepreneurial empire. It was the 90's. The big .COM boom. People were making their money with that, and I wanted to do the same. I wanted to be one of them.

Gradually, I realized I was wrong.

After a handful of years in practice, I made the connection that the law was my business, alongside the title agency that I had. I was looking for something outside of the profession of law to be my business and finally I came to the conclusion, the realization: The law was my business.

I needed to treat it like a business.

Nurture it like a business.

Succeed by working my way up the food chain from practitioner of the law, to marketer of the law, to owner of the law firm. That was how I'd be an entrepreneur.

By now, I've stacked multiple trips down entrepreneurial paths. I've got my bumps, my bruises, and my beautiful views. Let me share a few lessons that can serve as trail markers for anyone else about to brave those trails.

FOCUS ON THE GAIN, NOT THE GAP.

We're always setting goals for ourselves to create a direction, but when we to start seeing resistance, or lack of traction, we get discouraged at falling short.

"Hey, I'm not getting there."

"I didn't make a million dollars this year."

"I wrote down on paper I was going to make a million dollars this year."

"Damn it."

"Why didn't I do it?"

What I'm not looking at, in that example, is the fact I did increase revenue by 25%. I put things in place. The ingredients are there. Goals tend to be outcome based, rather than the output needed to obtain the outcome. With the right output, the right ingredients, the outcome you want will manifest. A rampant point-of-view in modern society, not isolated to the legal profession, is "less than" talk.

"I've got a good law firm, but I don't have *their* great law firm."
"I've got a nice car, but I don't have *their* great car."
"I've got a nice suit but I don't have—" *-you get it?*

In your early years you get those first big paydays. You start trying to fill the gap you see between yourself and other people you want to be. Let me tell you, from experience, it's a slippery slope. The time comes when you can buy that nicer car, wear that nicer suit, take that nicer trip, but because you spent so much time and energy focusing on the thing you don't have the "less than" mindset still exists.

You have the things, but you don't have the contentment. I'm not insinuating in the slightest that you shouldn't have scalable goals but an attitude of gratitude along the way is going to do wonders for your peace of mind, and keep you centered on that essential quality that will keep you grounded: humility.

Especially when you're on the journey towards building your business, mindfully cultivate a sense of where you are in the present. Really take in where you are, versus where you started. Contentment is built a lot around recognition, and a practice of gratitude. Recognize the grass is not always greener on the other side. Be content. Be humble. Otherwise you'll barrel past your finish line without ever realizing you crossed it.

There are still plenty of professional goals I want to achieve in my life but for myself. I end my day with a Bombay sapphire martini. That's my finish line. That's my reminder that I've made it.

Focus on the gains, not the goal.

WHERE FOCUS GOES, ENERGY FLOWS.

I'm borrowing this phrase from Tony Robbins. It's proven to be true in my experience. It's mind boggling what happens when you follow it as one of your core principles.

I feel this is an important building block to add to the previous maxim. When you're fixated on an outcome, it's easier to adopt a *by any means* sort of mantra.

"No matter what, I'm going to get there."

That tenacity is good. That drive is good. But if your focus is fixed on the destination, it's easy to become farsighted and miss critical pieces of the journey along the way. We spend so much focus on those big, life changing goals and accomplishments that we never contemplate what's on the other side. After all, if you're lucky, there's plenty of life on the other side of achievement. A critical question, after you've hit those goals and secured everything you could want is:

What next?

When I was 54, I was in a coaching group that I was blessed to be selected for. We were working with the book *Becoming a Resident Leader.* I was going through the exercise and, for the first time, I recognized my blessings. I realized just how good I had it. I was nowhere near a position where I wanted to throttle back. Money was taking care of itself. Everything was good. I was on the greener grass, and I needed something more. This time, it wasn't that "less-than" sort of more which trips lawyers up seeking things that change their individual lives. I wanted to change other lives. I wanted to make a difference. I wanted to change the world. I needed a mission. So I meditated.

MARCH TO A MILLION

What followed was my March to a Million. I decided, before I reached the age of 65 on September 30, 2030, I was going to positively impact one million lives. It became a central motivating force in my work. It transformed my life. What started as an individual goal turned into a team goal through my work with Wealth Strategies Network. It grew broader and broader.

The clients I helped were part of my million.
The people I employed, were part of my million.
Anyone who read a blog post and was influenced were part of my million.

I started seeing the number climb too fast. I said to myself, "This isn't going to work." So then I moved to a more individual focused frame of mind. It had to be a more direct interaction. A direct type of connection. I had to change one life at a time. The numbers started to climb back down and the hard work began. Compassionate contact with a million people.

Being an entrepreneur is nothing less than looking for how to make the job that much harder on yourself, right?

MOVING THE GOAL POST

That's the work, though. That's the delicate dance. It's easy to lean into the gain rather than the goal and lose momentum. It's easy to focus on the destination and let the present pass you by. The hard work though, the good work, is being mindful enough to honor both so that when you reach the next level you have everything in place to move the goal post.

Move the goal. For my march to a million, it led me to expand my team, redefine the numbers, and integrate with Wealth Strategies Network. It crystallized what I wanted to do. It became about impacting a million families and preventing them from suffering unnecessary financial loss.

It also really solidified the mindset of "Who, not How?"

You own your own firm. You own your own business. You're simultaneously your own accountant, marketer, and manager. Your head hanging heavy from all the hats you're wearing and you're ending every day wondering, "How the heck am I going to get this done?"

Instead of focusing on the *how*, focus on the *who.*

Delegating tasks to people with the proper skillset is game-changing. The leverage of figuring out who can get it done for you, the power that concept can bring to your business is exponential. Instead of focusing on how the heck you get something done, put your focus on who is the right person for this specific task?

I said to myself, if I build this team with the work we expect to have in mind, we'll be able to take care of a lot of people. We'll have an infrastructure where a sort of automation happens after a while. We'll get to a million and, when we do, then we're going on to ten.

STANDARD OF CARE

I had an epiphany many years ago while in Scottsdale, Arizona on day two of a three-day trust litigation deposition. I was working with several other attorneys, receiving $250 an hour, and I was by far the cheapest of the lot. Something was really gnawing at me. It festered through dinner and well into my evening martini. It occurred to me that the family I was serving reminded me a lot of my family. An entrepreneurial patriarch, who made some money and set up an estate, passed away leaving everything to the mother who struggled to manage everything left behind.

When she decided she wanted to change things she assembled a financial advisor, an insurance guy, a tax guy, a lawyer, but she lacked a relationship with all of them. They treated her like a transaction, like a payday. She couldn't bring herself to trust them. She ended up leaning on her son who, instead of doing things the right way, listened to what she wanted, with I'm sure the best of intentions, but opened the door to a lot of hardship. What followed was a bull-in-a-china-shop litigation process. The soon-to-be-disinherited charities, who were paying for several of those lawyers, didn't like what was happening. A million dollars or so later, the family loses and settles in court. If Mom had a professional she could truly rely on, a professional she had a relationship with and could trust, all of that could be prevented.

People, especially in times of crisis,
will lean on trust over expertise.

That particular instance is what started my journey into estate planning. It aligned with the core of what I wanted to do. I hated the transactional nature of it, so I ultimately decided I wanted to bring as much value into those relationships as I could by learning tools to separate the wheat from the chaff. I wanted to protect people from the malarkey that's out there in the financial world.

So I set on a path, taking a sabbatical from my practice, and spent the next three years learning the ins and outs of Financial Planning. It affirmed a lot of what I didn't like, looking at it from the outside. I've spent the past fifteen years building financial businesses to marry the financial and legal sides into a completely independent business. I found a way to move forward, leveraging the network I built, the tools I've acquired, and shortening the learning curve for attorneys who, like me, want to be the single point of responsibility to insure the best outcome for their clients.

For me, it's a standard of care.

If I sat across the table from a family that had more than $600,000 in assets, we'd be talking about AB trust to protect them against a 35% and up estate tax. A vast majority of people who are sitting across from estate planning lawyers face equal or worse tax problems with regard to their IRAs.

They're sitting there across the table from a guy with a million dollar IRA that's going to lose $300,000 of it to taxes and they say, "I can't do anything about that. That's the financial guy's job."

If I have my way, of making this movement where this is now the norm, that sort of abdication of responsibility will become malpractice. Individual consumers are going to get clocked if they don't get good advice.

We are the last foot soldiers to be able to provide this unbiased information and guidance. It's only going to become more difficult for the consumer to get good information in the future and take action, because they can get all kinds of information. Information leads to inaction, which in this instance, leads to financial loss.

ALCHEMY IN ACTION:

Focus on the gain, not the gap: Celebrate the small successes on the way to achieving larger goals.

Where focus goes, energy flows: Keep your focus on the work in front of you, rather than the big picture or goal post.

Standard of care: Insure the best outcome for your clients

CLAIM $729 IN FREE RESOURCES
TO GET MORE CLIENTS, RECLAIM YOUR TIME, AND BUILD YOUR IDEAL LAW FIRM...

Add fuel to your entrepreneurial fire with our collection of guides, templates, and how-to information, guaranteed to help you:

- Generate high-quality, pre-sold leads for your law firm (so you can stop worrying about whether or not the phone is going to ring this week)

- Improve your leadership skills through superior communication techniques (which translate just as well to communication with a spouse or partner)

- Take back control of your marketing (including how to communicate with and hold your vendors accountable)

- Develop a stronger brand message (with a big, bold promise)

- Master your core financial numbers (so your firm runs like a well-oiled, profit-generating machine instead of a "what's happened lately" patchwork of decisions)

- And more!

This package of resources is exclusively for readers of this book, and to claim yours, just go to:

WWW.LAWFIRMALCHEMY.COM/VOLUME1

Go right now to get your hands on these free gifts for you!

chapter 11

FINANCIAL PATHWAYS TO FREEDOM
WITH LEAH MILLER

Leah Miller, of LNM Financial Services, has years of experience as an in-house law firm Chief Financial Officer. She offers fractional CFO and bookkeeping service, expanding her reach, and helping small businesses, to aid clients on their journey to financial health. She has mastered improving financial operations by providing strategic guidance, managing cash flow, and analyzing financial data to identify opportunities for growth and movement.

MOST BUSINESS OWNERS DREAD talking about finance. They're creatives. They're entrepreneurs. They're content to let the accountants and number crunchers sort the money, as long as there's enough in the bank.

They're missing out.

Finance is just as important to your law firm's long-term growth as how you advertise and how you operate. You can run your business without ever really knowing how to read a financial statement, but you're denying yourself the chance to acquire some really incredible tools to run your business more efficiently.

I have always loved numbers and talking about numbers and the finance part of everything. I've kind of always geeked out about taxes and things like that.

I was a firm administrator for a personal injury law firm for eight years. I climbed the ladder from paralegal to administrator before reaching the top of the ladder as the firm's Chief Financial Officer. I've always loved understanding money, and how it informs our future. Now I work with a variety of law firms, and more often than not I find finance is the last thing people think about. If the money is coming in, and the cases are coming in, and there's enough money to make payroll, then people really aren't worried about it.

If people paid a little more attention to finance, they can see how it can make the work they do, whether it's marketing or operations, even stronger.

ACCOUNTING FOR THE BIG PICTURE

For a lot of law firms, pay days are months in the making. If you're a personal injury firm, things are twelve to eighteen months out for almost everything. You're waiting for big cases to go to trial, and in between you're fronting the cost to operate. Not only do you not have income coming in from the case you're working on, but you're also sometimes accumulating tens of thousands of dollars in costs you're going to have to recoup when the money does finally come in.

Being able to know how much you have coming down the line is invaluable information. It gives you clarity. It gives you security. It helps your vision. In my career I've seen $10,000 dollar cases become multimillion dollar cases, and I've seen million-dollar cases get devalued to thousand dollar cases. Knowing where you are with your expected cashflow can really help weather those peaks and valleys and navigate your operating costs and your variable expenses. Personal injury has a lot of ups and downs. It's feast or famine in a way totally distinct from other types of legal practices. Having a grip on your money can really bolster your longevity.

There are a lot of catalysts for disruption. Having a firm understanding of money, beyond what's in the bank to make payroll, can help make those decisions for how to handle the law firm.

BACK TO BASICS

It's an easy sentiment: **Know your money.** The more helpful question is: **How?**

If I were airdropped into a personal injury firm doing around $2-3 million a year, gross, there are several steps I would take to help get them organized.

It's all about going **back to basics**.

The first step is to find what's missing. What does book-keeping look like? How is accounting? What's the method of keeping records for returns for the past five years? Etc. Etc. Etc.

It's how I got started in this line of work, so I still do it independently for firms to this day. A lot of people just leave it to their CPA to handle the numbers. CPA's are essential for tax reasons, but they're not always handling your bookkeeping and accounting in a way to best equip you to make strategic decisions. It's really beneficial to understand your bookkeeping beyond the scope of tax reasons and compliance.

Go back to basics. Take a look at your fundamental operational and financial structures, with a curious mind, make sure they're serving your business. Are you keeping track of everything on your profit and loss as a way to make clear decisions? How do you differentiate wages?

I see a lot of times wages are just broadly listed as wages. This lack of specificity isn't helping your bookkeeping. Split wages into categories. Split officer wages, associate attorney wages, and paralegal wages. Break them down. It provides clarity. It tells you when things are going well and case costs are being recouped. It also tells us when things might need to change.

Once the basics are in place and we have a good idea of the situation with bookkeeping, the next thing I'd turn my attention to are goals.

What are your goals?

I have some clients who simply want to be comfortable. That's an amazing goal. There's nothing wrong with just wanting to go home at five o'clock, and being able to comfortably provide for the lifestyle you want. I have other clients with further-reaching goals. They want to expand. They want to cultivate a distinct culture of performance in their firm. No matter what the goal is, it takes money. The next step in the process is clearly defining goals, and what needs to happen in order to obtain them. Determining goals determines the steps, and determining the steps helps establish our budget.

If you have a good system in place, it doesn't have to be complex or overwhelming. Developing techniques to utilize financial documents, bookkeeping, and accounting will put you above the curve. Do it while you don't have to and prevent the stress that comes from a day when you need to.

PROFIT AND LOSS

A seemingly easy yet remarkably complex document that's worth utilizing is the Profit and Loss (or PNL) statement. You have to do it right. An old boss of mine used to say, **"Garbage in, garbage out."**

If you put the wrong information into your systems, you're going to get the wrong information back. It's going to be useless to you. The P&L shows your gross revenue, all of your expenses, and your net profit. Organize your P&L in an easily digestible way. It should be clear.

Once you do, refer back to it periodically to make sure you are spending money where it needs to be spent. I'm talking beyond marketing and office supplies. What's your spending on meals? Entertainment? What is the average cost of travel expenses? There are a lot of different parts that are worth periodically looking at and asking,

"Is this a necessary, worthwhile expense?"

You may find places to change, or ways your money could be better spent. Another thing I like to do on the P&L is look at case costs. We want to be stewards of the client's money, and not waste it unnecessarily. The client's happiness, and their outcome, is the bottom line.

SCALING YOUR PRACTICE

I'm a huge advocate for contract-based employment. There's a lot more to full-time compensation than just base salary. Especially if you're not familiarizing yourself with your P&L, it's easy to overlook the extra cost in money and time to train somebody. Bringing on an experienced contract attorney can really help accelerate your momentum.

Hiring on a fractional basis helps scale your practice. There's a whole world of virtual paralegals who are amazing at what they do. They've been doing it for years and you can get it at a fraction of the cost. I'm still big on hiring locally if it's important to a firm's values. However, looking at these new and innovative options can help stretch your money and resources to invest where it's really needed.

Looking for individuals outside your firm to fulfill specific tasks doesn't only apply to attorneys and paralegals, but to almost every level of your business. It's the core of my work as a Fractional CFO. Bringing on a full-time CFO costs a lot of money. A fractional CFO looks at the future of your financials.

They can do the budgeting, work on KPIs, forecast your cash flow and, above all, help define your future. It's an incredible option to utilize a specific service for, no pun intended, a fraction of what a full-time role would cost.

FEAR OF GROWTH

I have some clients who are in growth phases. They can hire certain positions but there are still some goals they need to reach before they complete their starting lineup. What's key, to me, is to be conservative enough with your financials so there is a constant buffer in place so you never have to stress about making payroll. We want to make sure that we're leaving a buffer of cash flow rather than overextending ourselves.

When firm owners look ahead to their financial future there is not only anxiety about not having enough, but also a certain anxiety from having more than you've ever had before. There's a fear that comes from feeling inadequate, or ill-equipped, to manage all of it. If you're making six figures, hiring staff, and looking ahead to managing seven figures or a multi-million-dollar firm, there's a real fear of stepping out into the unknown. It's unfamiliar. It's an alien sort of success.

Firm owners went to law school to master their craft, to practice law. The idea of having to cultivate an understanding of business and finance can be daunting to a lot of lawyers. A lot of my clients struggle with finding the balance.

It's where an outside eye can help you. Find a good CPA. Hire a Fractional CFO. Get excited about your financial future. Most importantly, **don't skimp on finance.**

Money is a taboo subject for a lot of people, but if you take time to understand it, it can save you so much time and stress. Once you have that understanding, and processes in place, there's a real freedom and peace you can acquire. Take an hour out of your month. Make the numbers make sense. Ensure you're making the right decision. It will put you ahead if you're starting out. Develop a firm foundation.

Understand that the more a firm grows, the more you lose touch with finance. It's natural, and necessary, to take your hands off the wheel. It will be the case with marketing, day-to-day operations, and finance too. Those responsibilities will eventually be in the hands of a full-time CFO and an operations manager. If you develop a firm foundation early, it's going to equip you down the road to make the most strategic hire when the time comes to fill those positions. Bringing someone in to handle your financials is a massive act of trust. Equip yourself to make the best decision when the time comes.

ALCHEMY IN ACTION:

Account for the big picture: Familiarize yourself with finance as a means to achieving your goals.

Profit and loss: Monitor where your money is going and make sure it is working for you.

Scaling your practice: Consider hiring on a fractional basis as a means of scaling your practice.

chapter 12

BUILD YOUR FIRM, NOT SOMEONE ELSE'S
— CHARLEY

EVERYONE KNOWS the platitude. It comes from Oscar Wilde. What people don't realize is that it's only half of the infamous quote. The full quote is, **"Imitation is the sincerest form of flattery that mediocrity can pay to greatness."**

Boom. Pen drop. Quill drop. Whatever Wilde wrote with, it was a long time ago.

A lot goes wrong when we focus on imitation instead of innovation.

The first issue you run into is a flimsy business model. It becomes easier to punch holes in the business model because it doesn't quite fit you. It sounds great when we first hear about it but, once we try to implement it, we write it off immediately when it doesn't work. **You fall into the trap of memorizing tactics instead of understanding principles.**

When we look at law firms that have a lot going on, most of the time we're getting an outside perspective. We are glimpsing the externals of the machine. We aren't seeing how the machine operates. Within every great law firm is a system of substructures, and bigger reasons, why the business model works. When we try to copy that, we're going off of the outside perspective. We're copying the external, and not the inner-workings which make the external so alluring.

You can paint a car red and call it a Ferrari, but if you don't have what counts under the hood, you aren't fooling anyone.

You can't do a one for one duplication. Every firm operates with different data sets, ethics, and is built for its own market.

Every firm is unique. Every firm should be optimized to thrive in its specific market. You have to equip your firm with exactly what you need to thrive in yours.

We live in such a culture of comparison. We latch onto what someone else is doing and wish we could do the same. Remember you became a lawyer to fulfill your dream, not someone else's. You should absolutely be learning from other firm owners. There is no substitute for having people within the industry to communicate with, collaborate with, and to mastermind with.

Those connections exist to inform who you need to grow into, not how to mold you into someone else's version of who you think you should be.

FIND THE RIGHT COACH

A good coach can help to toe the line between finding inspiration and seeking imitation. Yes, I am absolutely an advocate for the idea of coaches knowing full well that I am a coach.

A coach helps you see the big picture. Having someone in your corner who is continuously absorbing the structures and substructures surrounding these decisions keeps you grounded. It keeps you growing. You can begin to understand your firm from a holistic perspective.

It's another easy trap to fall into if you try to recreate someone else's firm. That other firm isn't taking stock of your needs. They're not looking at your firm or finding potential potholes. They're not zooming out to look at the big picture. They're focused on their own big picture, It's not their responsibility to help you get where you want your business to be. They're running their law firm.

If they're selling a package offering an inside look at their firm? Amazing. Take advantage of it. You'll come out with brand new lessons, brand new ideas, and inspiration. It's valuable. But then you have to digest what you've learned and figure out how it fits into your plan, your vision, your dream.

The same thing applies with marketing strategies. Marketing strategies vary. They vary from market to market and community to community. If you tried to copy one set of those strategies and paste them into a different market, you'd likely not see a return on investment.

UNDERSTAND WHAT YOU REALLY WANT

What type of firm do you want to run? What do you want your story to be? I'm not talking about the practice area. I mean big picture. I'm talking about simple steps.

Take inventory of where you are right now, in this moment. Ask yourself:

> *Am I building a lifestyle business? Am I building*
> *an empire? Am I building something in between?*
> *What is available in my existing market?*
> *Where's the ceiling? The market cap?*

The market cap is always bigger than most perceive, but there still are potential market caps in your area depending on the practice. What are you really trying to build? I would even say, what do you want your day and your week to feel like?

This is a critical exercise I do with all of my coaching clients. A while back, I was going back and forth with one of my clients about their vision. Revenue growth was certainly a part of it, but they were really struggling to pin down what revenue growth meant to them.

One day, they sent me a message saying,

"If I'm being 100% honest, I really want to be able to leave the office every day at 5:00 pm. I want to have the energy for family and friends. I want to join a country club and, every Friday, play a round with a referral source."

They began talking about the lifestyle they wanted versus how much they wanted their revenue to grow. Their struggle was determining how much money they needed to make for the firm to afford their ideal lifestyle. An opportunity arose.

If they needed to make a certain amount of money, what did it represent in terms of profit? Their desire to have a certain lifestyle meant needing to grow their firm, which scared them.

I don't cite this example to toot my coaching horn, or even to tell you what happened next, but rather to highlight the circular frame of mind where we ask the question, "Am I asking too much?"

We live in a comparison culture. Empire attorneys envy lifestyle attorneys. It doesn't matter if your firm is six, or seven figures. It's easy to get this artificial, grandiose view of everything and convince yourself what you have is nothing.

It's so important to figure out what works best for you, not just what you want but how you want to go about chasing it. I have no interest in judging someone else's journey. It drives me crazy when I hear people devalue other people for not chasing what society says you should be chasing.

I believe in doing what you are passionate about and what your focus is calling you to spend your energy on. It is far more compelling to go through life being deeply focused than to spend all of your energy 'keeping up with the Jones.

ADOPT AND ADAPT

When you are deep in the passionate work of constructing something, you can easily spend eight hours investing and completely ignoring the rest of the world. At the end of the day it's not about the money. It's about doing something you love. That was the takeaway from the text exchange I had with my client. If all of those things are in place, the money will be there. Money facilitates the journey.

When I'm working with people, I focus on how they can build their business so they are the owner, rather than being owned by their practice. It's a major, dynamic shift. **Who owns who? Do you own the practice or does the practice own you?** In times where I see people focus on recreation of someone else's firm, the practice tends to own them. In abdicating the responsibility of building for themselves, they lose their vision by jealously looking at what other people have.

Cultivate a curiosity of how firms operate and, rather than copying and pasting, a phrase I like to use is **adopt and adapt**.

When you adopt and adapt, you can recognize what you build. You can grow your practice, while always understanding how it works. I'm going to be capable of teaching these systems, building more systems on top of them, and understanding how my practice really works.

Study models, have mentors, but don't copy their path step by step because of where they landed. At the end of the day, if you just keep trying to reconstruct someone else's firm you will always be able to poke holes in it. You will always be an outsider in your own practice.

The great companies of the world don't duplicate each other. They learn from each other. They study each other. They model some of the things that their peers do.

You're in the business of figuring out your culture, your goals, your ideal life, and constructing it. When you know what you're doing, life is gratifying every day. You deserve to be excited about where you are going. You deserve to live your individual dream. Don't just be content with where you are on the journey to someone else's dream. Be excited about where you get to go on the road to your dream.

ALCHEMY IN ACTION:

Build your own firm: Understand principles rather than memorizing tactics.

Understand what you really want: Determine what you are really trying to build.

chapter 13

SEVEN FIGURE MARKETING
WITH CASSIDY LEWIS

Cassidy Lewis is the Chief Marketing Officer at Cooper Hurley Injury Lawyers. Known as "The Car Crash Experts", the firm is located in Hampton Roads Virginia, with nine locations throughout the region. Using her years of experience and knowledge, gained through her bachelor's and master's degrees, Mrs. Lewis has led the marketing and branding efforts of the firm for over 6 years. She is most proud of bringing her partner's marketing vision to life with her team.

I KNOW LAWYERS, and a conclusion I've come to, watching the attorneys in my office, is that when the time comes to get creative, lawyers have learned some habits worth unlearning.

In law school, you're taught to pick everything apart. It's a skill you need, especially in building an argument. Careful analysis makes for great attorneys and can become a huge obstacle in marketing.

When dealing with the creative process, over-analysis can get in the way. It's stifling for the creatives and marketers in your workplace.

As creatives, you're taught to lean into saying "yes". Creativity involves building ideas up, whereas the law involves picking things apart to break down concepts. The two can be at odds with one another, but when they work in tandem? Beautiful things can happen.

This chapter is about how to switch off your attorney brain for a bit and put on the creative lens to make you dynamic, and incredibly successful, in your marketing.

NEVER LET PERFECT GET IN THE WAY OF GOOD

Think about all of the strategy, all of the campaigns, and all of the deadlines fast approaching in your world. If we picked them apart, we would work at it all day and nothing would get off the ground. Rather than focusing on a perfectly polished product, allow your creatives to strategize. Allow your marketers to market. Allow them to be tactical. Allow them to fail!

Save your lawyer lens for the areas you shine and trust your creatives to work their process.

Learn the value of never letting perfect get in the way of good. That bit of advice might seem simple but believe me I understand how difficult it can be to relinquish control of something that's important to you. Something you've obtained through a lot of hard work. However, that simple bit of advice could literally save your professional relationship with your creative partners.

It's critical.

Learning how to work with your creatives isn't just a positive skill to add to your tool belt, it's an essential one. Understanding both sides helps a lot. So let's take a second to better understand the marketer in your office, so we can better equip ourselves to work with them.

YOUR MARKETER AND YOU

Marketers are the oddballs in the office, especially an office filled with attorneys. They think differently. They speak differently. Their energy is different. So, there are two things that are extremely important for the marketer in your office.

The first thing is regular, consistent communication. When attorneys have to fill in the blank, they begin to pick apart the work and stall the creative process.

The second thing, and brace yourself, because I'm gonna use a buzzword but it's extremely important, we need the budget. There, I said it. I said the b-word. I speak to legal marketers and ask,

"What's your annual budget? What's your monthly budget?" And so often they come back with:

"Oh, well, I just tell him or her, this is what I want to do, and I get this project approved."

I can't do anything about that. I want out. I'm crying, I'm screaming because I can only be tactical. I can't strategize. I don't know what's happening next month. I'm fearful every time I have to ask you for money. There's anxiety, and anxiety is death to creativity.

If you want to be a leader in your office, those baby steps are so important. Communication and a clear budget are essential for me to do my work well.

MEET WITH YOUR MARKETERS

If you're either a firm owner or a marketer and you need to establish a type of rhythm, where should you begin?

Start by setting aside a full day for the marketer and managing partner to meet. If there are multiple partners, a full day meeting with the marketer and two or three shareholders.

One full day, it could be two! It's more about intention than it is about time. You're assessing your strengths. You're talking about marketing strategies. You communicate the larger vision of the firm; where you want to be in two to three years. Ten years, Twenty. That time communicating will save you so much time and energy on the other side. Take the first day and figure out where your marketer's strengths lie and where the business owners and the law firm owners actually want to go.

When you think of marketing as a law firm owner, narrow your top three marketing priorities, rather than focusing on everything. Maybe it's social. Maybe it's a podcast, a YouTube channel. Don't make it everything. Figure out those big picture strategies. Figure out the 'why' behind it. I love a good SWOT (Strength, Weaknesses, Opportunities and Threats) analysis. I know there are newer versions, but I still love a SWOT analysis.

I have them every year in my marketing playbook, or my marketing plan, just to figure out what the strategy is going to be for the next two to three years.

TRANSPARENCY

Everyone, whether you're a marketer, a manager, or a lawyer, has qualities in themselves that inspire trust from others. For myself, it's transparency. I'm transparent with others, and transparent with myself. There's little distinction between the two. I can be just as hard on myself as I am with the people I work with. I expect the same of myself as I would of them. If I mess something up, I am going to bring it to someone before they can bring it to me.

I'm an empath. I'm a natural people pleaser. It's helped me build a community around myself, but it's also exhausting. It can cause anxiety. It can lead to burnout. It can lead to pleasing no one, including myself.

I've struggled with feelings of unworthiness. So as a response, I've created this abundance of transparency. From there, we build trust. Sometimes, trust comes from upsetting people and upsetting the status quo.

Not everybody approaches it the same way. I think transparency is beneficial when you're working with a firm owner who is heavy on the litigation side. They're looking for the pattern which would upset them and would give them reason to say something isn't working. They're a walking SWOT analysis with a heavy emphasis on the W and the T.

The point is, if you are a marketer in a firm, transparency is transformative. It means you're not going to have stuff picked apart in the same way, because there isn't a constant concern to find the truth. The truth is always present.

BUILDING TRUST WITH DATA

After communication and transparency, the other side of building trust is a data driven approach. When you're talking with colleagues about data, what should firms be tracking? What is the information you are tracking to aid in the development of marketing? In growth? In building trust?

Consider this exercise with your team. When you sit down for the big meeting between your marketers and your leaders, discuss together what pieces of data could serve as impartial evidence your creative team is on the right track? What are the KPI's, or Key Performance Indicators, that count for you?

One of the more powerful KPIs I've been tracking over the last two years are conversion rates. Specifically, conversion rates within referral sources. Television is definitely one of the more expensive referral sources, but it has a higher conversion rate. Everything else is converting at about 25%.

Television is converting at 40%.

What information does that give us? What does it mean for us? When I use the term conversion rate, I mean qualified leads that could and should become clients. Someone who called for a personal injury case with enough qualifiers in place for our firm to handle. Meaning, 40% of people who call from television ads are qualified to work with our firm.

THE THREE TENANTS OF MARKETING

There are three primary duties of someone in marketing. The first is to make the phone ring with what I call green intakes, intakes that we want.

Number two is to empower all of our internal and external resources to make the phone ring with the right intakes, the green intakes. The third, and final piece, is branding. As you can imagine, branding is the most difficult to measure. We use what's called the Marshall Marketing Report. They look at brand recall for regions by industry. So they ask 10,000 people who live in a region and say,

"If you had to name a personal injury lawyer, who would you name?"

What I measure is how much we are named. Afterwards, we look at who was mentioned ahead of us and figure out a strategy based on what they are doing.

ESTABLISHING THE RIGHT TEAM

One of the things complicating so much of the work law firms are doing is the failure to staff up the marketing team. It's essential to know the things to look for when assembling your team of creatives.

The marketing industry is fragmented. Your marketing senior leadership needs to be the most well-versed in the three different pieces of the industry. Second, you want to build a team out of your deficiencies. You want people to thrive where you struggle. That's going to establish solid checks and balances.

The key to successful marketing is clear, transparent communication; a team whose strengths check others' weaknesses, the space and room to be creative, and the openness to have it questioned and analyzed. If you can get that combination, you're golden.

ALCHEMY IN ACTION:

Communicate clearly: Focus on the importance of clear and consistent communication between the marketing team and the managing partner.

Match your budget with your goals: Set a marketing budget that aligns with the firm's goals.

Build trust: Determine what creates trust in your team.

Let the numbers do the talking: Be data driven, and let it inform your strategies.

Build a balanced team: Form a team where strengths check weaknesses.

GROWING YOUR BUSINESS
WITH RYAN MCKEEN

Ryan McKeen is a nationally recognized attorney based in Connecticut who has received numerous accolades for his work in personal injury law. He has been honored by the Connecticut Personal Injury Hall of Fame for securing one of the highest settlements in the state. The Connecticut Law Tribune named him in the Personal Injury Hall of Fame. His former firm was a finalist in the Motorcyclist category, having achieved one of the highest settlements or verdicts in a wrongful death action in a motorcycle case.

His successful cases and honors, such as being named a Super Lawyer and a New Leader in The Law, speak to his competence and dedication. Beyond his legal prowess, McKeen's empathetic approach is noteworthy. He understands the plight of victims, having himself experienced the trials of a personal injury incident. Furthermore, his commitment to making law accessible, demonstrated through his blog and books, ensures that clients are well-informed and empowered throughout their legal journey. Coupled with his community service and dedication to ethical practice, McKeen offers not just legal

> *representation, but also a partnership rooted in trust, transparency, and unwavering advocacy.*
>
> *In 2016, Ryan was included in the Hartford Business Journal's "40 under 40" list, which recognizes promising young professionals in the Hartford area. He has been recognized by his peers as a Super Lawyer.*

FOR MANY the definition of success is too small. This is especially true with lawyers. In law school, you are constantly competing against your peers. You're graded on a curve. There are only so many spots on different journals. There are only a select number of spots on a moot court team. It's survival of the fittest and only the select few are going to cross that finish line. It's part tradition and it's part training. I also just think it's economically advantageous for the powers that be. A scarcity mindset maintains a certain status quo.

It continues once we make it out into the real world. You get a clerkship with a certain judge, or maybe go to work at a bigger firm and that's what success looks like. You get taught this is the only way. You're a failure otherwise. It causes people to stick in a job they shouldn't stick in. Law Schools feed into that system, into that version of success. It's so tiny. The reality is there are ample opportunities for success in the law profession. There are ample ways to succeed. Before us, there is an absolute abundance.

I'm the first person in my family to graduate from a four-year college. I was so happy to be a lawyer. I wanted to help people. I came out of law school, and I worked at a small general practice local firm. These kinds of firms are closing up nowadays, if they even exist in your town. We were a one-stop shop for the community. You got a DUI? You called us. Car accident? You called us? Will? Divorce? There we were. I was generating revenue and I did good work, but it was always about keeping the latter in mind over the former.

I went to law school to try to help people. I wanted to be the person who helped solve problems. I never wanted to work for big companies. I didn't want to work for the government. It didn't interest me. I wanted experience. I was able to gain that experience through a very small firm at a very early age. It really helped me in my career. Chasing after the experiences that fit my version of success, versus society's, gave me a clear idea of what to do next and the trajectory I wanted for my life.

LEARN TO BE UNCOMFORTABLE

It was a great gift to me. When you're working for a small firm, you have to learn the basics of business.

You have to learn how to generate clients. You have to learn intake. You have to know how to manage a case, from start to finish.

You have to be willing to be uncomfortable.

You have to get used to an uphill climb. Every day you have to go out and make arguments. You are constantly challenging yourself. It's not a comfortable life. If you are in a small law firm, you are going to learn the ins and outs of running a business more than you ever could at a multi-million-dollar firm equipped with a staff of specialists to help carry the load. That discomfort will make you better.

The ability to go out and learn the law, to learn from good lawyers, and to start building a practice was incredibly attractive to me.

How does someone get comfortable with discomfort? Can discomfort turn into a crucible of potential energy that spits you out the other side, better than you were before?

I think it is a muscle, something you exercise. Everyone has varying degrees of threshold, a limit to how much they can reach out of their comfort zone. It's about exercising your resolve, your patience, to constantly push past your comfort zone.

As you do it, you start to build up muscle. You start to build up strength. There's no secret to it. There will be nerves. There will be sleepless nights. There will be over-prepping and under-prepping. There will be self-doubt. There will be impostor syndrome.

There will be progress. There will be growth.

There's no substitute for going out there, doing the thing, and pushing through.

GROWING YOUR OWN FIRM

I worked for my small firm for six and a half years. I was 32 years old and, while on a trip to the Bahamas, I devoured a biography on Steve Jobs. I realized I was being way too conservative with my life and my potential. I couldn't keep living the same year or doing the same work, over and over. I needed to fulfill a higher purpose. I needed to take a risk.

What started as a revelation in the Caribbean, fueled by possibly one too many Bahama mamas, would become another uphill climb to branch out on my own. I had several failed attempts, several partnerships, and several close-calls falling out with friends, but what came from all of it was a dynamic, financially successful trial firm which carried me through the next decade.

You learn a lot of lessons in ten years of growing a practice, particularly business lessons. If I had a time machine and hopped back ten years to give 32 year old Ryan some advice, this would be it.

When you're starting a business, **set it up right**. Set it up to succeed. Plan for success. Get your books in order from day one. Invest in software to help you grow. Adopt a mindset of doing what is not only best for today, but best for what your business is going to grow into. Lay the foundation.

The next bit of advice is to **be very intentional about the work you want to do**. Do the vision work for your firm. A great book I recommend for anyone who wants a starting point is *Traction: Get a Grip on Your* **Business by Geno Wickman**. I can't recommend the book enough. Read the first 75 pages, and even if you don't go beyond it, set the vision for your business.

Identify your ideal client.

Identify the work you want to do.

Know what your values are.

Start developing and mapping out a ten year plan as to where it is that you want to be.

Next, **don't focus on what other people have that you don't.**

As you start, there are going to be people out there with way better marketing budgets, who appear way more successful. There will be people who have way more money, influence, even more talent than you.

Don't focus on that.

Focus on doing excellent work with what you have. Look at the clients you have. Get great results for them. Look at the work that you have and get better at it. So you don't have a 100-million-dollar paralysis case, but maybe you've got a $100,000 in a car accident case. Get the $100,000. Learn your craft. Make it a craft. Make it a practice.

Get Better. Get better at what you're doing.

SET IT UP RIGHT

I mentioned this briefly before but it merits some expansion. There are certain things that I wish I had done a lot earlier, things I thought weren't possible or were better suited down the road. Success is all about laying the infrastructure, putting the systems in place, to accommodate the level of success you envision for yourself. Two things I wish I had done earlier are hiring people outright and utilizing paid marketing.

I should have hired much earlier than I did. The idea of hiring was really scary for me. I didn't hire a full-time employee until I was six years into operating my business. I had a part-time assistant that worked nine hours a week but everything else I tackled myself. I did that for six years and, boy, did I cost myself a lot of money.

I never felt like I had the money to do it. I never felt comfortable enough. I was struggling to take home money as it was. I was working all the time, and I couldn't fathom finding enough extra money to support another salary in addition to mine.

However, the reason I wasn't making very much money was because I was doing tasks far beneath me. I was doing things that could have been done for ten dollars to fifteen dollars an hour and working nonstop. By putting so much on my plate I was capping up my top-level income. I should have made the leap much sooner. Fortunately, life stepped in and gave me no choice but to expand my team.

In September of 2017, we met Mikey Cruz. Mikey Cruz was paralyzed, through no fault of his own, as a result of his company failing to wrap light bulbs to a pallet in combination with a temporary worker operating a reach truck at a much lower level than he should have. That case would become a 100 million-dollar verdict that catapulted our business.

We knew we had to take it. I said, "Look, we have to build the firm to support this case. This is a big case. We've honed our skills. We don't want to refer the case out. We want to handle this case. We were meant to do this."

We were confident in our abilities. However, in order to get there, we needed a very good paralegal. We needed help. We also need somebody to do reception, and intake, and scan the mail. We can't afford to have all of our time eaten up by those things.

It stopped being about **I can't afford to hire someone to do this** to **I can't afford to spend time doing this myself.**

It completely changed how we viewed the workload. Once we had a paralegal and a receptionist, we realized we needed somebody to help us with workers comp, insurance and everything. So we brought in an office admin. So, in January of

2018, the firm went from me, my partner and my part time assistant, to adding three full time people in one month.

UTILIZE PAID MARKETING

Paying for marketing always felt out of reach. I have a news flash out there for anybody listening. Paid marketing works.

It is all pay for play. You pay cash or you pay with time. Looking back, I would have spent money purposely on marketing. I would have taken a percentage of my gross revenue and I would have said, "Here's what I anticipate for the year. Here's what I'm going to spend into marketing." And I would have made sure I spent it. I didn't do that.

Nowadays, the percentage of gross revenue we put back into marketing is very low to support where we are, but we don't have a problem generating good cases at this point. The bare minimum someone should put towards marketing is 6%, which is really the absolute floor. If you're making $100,000-$300,000 a year gross, devoting 12% of that into marketing can really help your firm grow faster

The more you spend, the faster you are going to see results. Set aside a percentage of gross revenue. I would set 6% as the absolute floor. I wouldn't recommend that. Above all, make sure you spend it. Don't allocate $18,000 this year for marketing, and then only use $1,200 because your Google Ad didn't perform well. Set the money aside and find a way to burn through it.

CULTIVATING A VISION

Working on a vision is the most important work you will do at your firm. In March of 2017, my partner Andrew and I sat down at a mid-level bar downtown with our *Traction* workbook and we got to work deciding who we were. We set our big, hairy, audacious goal to be a $10 million jury verdict firm. The reason why we sent that goal was that we wanted to be recognized as one of the top trial firms in Connecticut. That's what we wanted to be in ten years. That's what we wanted our future to look like. We didn't have a case worth $100,000 at that point but it didn't matter. We knew who we wanted to be.

I don't know if I would call it manifestation. I don't know what it is but we're putting out something that felt uncomfortable to us. We were exploring something that felt out of reach. It feels absurd, looking back, but what it did was determine what steps we were going to take next. It helped us find the hard questions to ask to figure out the best decisions to make. Shortly after, we found what would become our $100 million dollar case.

I've been fortunate to hang out with some incredibly successful people. The most successful people I know have the clearest visions for their companies, and themselves. They know the headcount. They know revenue. They know what it's going to look like, feel like, who their clients are going to be, and where they're going to come from, ten years from now to close.

Vision can also be fluid. If it's not working for you, maybe you're not in a place that you like more than anything else. You thought you wanted to marry this person, and it turns out that maybe you shouldn't have. Fine. Get a new vision. I think that's okay. Don't feel like you're getting married to what you need to be in ten years. Set the best vision you can for the time you're setting it. Once you start on the journey, the road will show you exactly where you need to go. It will show you what your version of success looks like.

Success takes work. It requires vision. It requires having the right people.

FINDING THE RIGHT PEOPLE

Hiring is the hardest thing about running a business. Even the biggest companies like Google, Microsoft and Amazon are batting 50%, at best. Even with the best people and resources it's a challenge, worldwide, to find and vet the best candidates. It is really imperfect. One thing I have learned in regard to hiring is to look beyond a candidate's resume and background and ask, "what is motivating this individual to work here?" That, to me, is critical. We look for candidates who see our firm as a step up from where they are. That is a great start.

They are happy to be here. We take it as a yellow flag if people see it as a lateral move. If you're taking a pay cut? It's a red flag. Skill level is important, but it's also who you are. You need to be recruiting top level talent, and that means skill and personality meshing perfectly.

If you are recruiting top level talent, it means taking the time to invest in them long before you offer them a job. Chances are the person you need to hire already has a job, with the potential of getting other jobs. That means developing a relationship over years. It means phone calls. It means lunches, or messages on

LinkedIn. It's about investing. Developing a relationship can take several years, even if you know right off the bat you want them to work with you. At the very top levels, it is about identifying talent in the market, going out, and recruiting.

Something I'm really into is stealth checking references. I rarely bother calling supplied references. Chances are people select individuals who are going to make them look good. I want a realistic glimpse into who you are in the workplace. I'm going to look for places where our work overlaps, find a shadow network of friends, or friends of friends, who can tell me who you are.

Hiring feels like a lot of cloak and dagger. You also have to make sure the person has the skillset for the job, and that means defining what skills are needed for the job that's open. This is a mistake I see a lot of law firms make. They have someone who is a great paralegal, or great with litigation, but terrible with intake and they put them in charge of office admin. These could be vastly different people. Don't assume a person may be immensely qualified and a good fit for one job in your organization, and not a fit for any other role in that organization. Define what it is you're hiring for, and look for things in their background that show they can do it. Learn their hobbies and their interests. Find out what other jobs they've had.

Are they detail oriented? Do they thrive working alone? They may be a great fit for your intake team. Are they creative? Find a place for them on the marketing team. Start defining your roles. Have multiple levels of interviews, because one of the things I've discovered is we have a tremendous bias in interviews. We have never gotten to a point where we have proactively hired. We are always reacting like we need somebody. The bias becomes just to hire out of pain, essentially. Whether

135

it's an existing person in that role or another lawyer in your firm, always have them interview and get some feedback from an outside perspective. As an owner, it's easy to develop a bias because of the pressure you feel to fill the role.

As a leader of your firm, you're like a combination of a teacher and a parent. What do teachers and parents do? They repeat themselves all the time. Never get tired of repeating this: growth allows us to create more opportunities. It allows us to promote people. It allows us to get better technology. It allows us to give bonuses, raises, and get better health care. If we're able to improve our team by adding people, don't shrink from it. A rising tide raises all boats.

ALCHEMY IN ACTION:

Embrace abundance: Develop your own vision of success and adopt an outlook of abundance.

Set it up right: Supply your business with the people, resources, and technology to match the vision you cultivate for success.

Develop a vision: Have a clear, and flexible vision for where you see yourself and your business three, five, and ten years from now.

Find the right people: Spend time cultivating relationships to hire top tier talent. Match skillsets to the skills of the job.

CLAIM $729 IN FREE RESOURCES
TO GET MORE CLIENTS, RECLAIM YOUR TIME, AND BUILD YOUR IDEAL LAW FIRM...

Add fuel to your entrepreneurial fire with our collection of guides, templates, and how-to information, guaranteed to help you:

- Generate high-quality, pre-sold leads for your law firm (so you can stop worrying about whether or not the phone is going to ring this week)

- Improve your leadership skills through superior communication techniques (which translate just as well to communication with a spouse or partner)

- Take back control of your marketing (including how to communicate with and hold your vendors accountable)

- Develop a stronger brand message (with a big, bold promise)

- Master your core financial numbers (so your firm runs like a well-oiled, profit-generating machine instead of a "what's happened lately" patchwork of decisions)

- And more!

This package of resources is exclusively for readers of this book, and to claim yours, just go to:

WWW.LAWFIRMALCHEMY.COM/VOLUME1

Go right now to get your hands on these free gifts for you!

chapter 15

$100 DOLLAR STARTUP
– CHARLEY

I GOT HOOKED ON A BOOK early on in my marketing journey. I was doing some freelance copywriting and marketing; It would still be another decade before I fully went into business for myself, but this book came across my desk and it was an eye-opener.

The book is *The $100 Startup: Reinvent the Way You Make a Living, Do What You Love, and Create a New Future* by Chris Guillebeau. It's incredible. It validated, for me, the idea that it really doesn't take a lot to get started. It's worth spending a chapter diving into this book, because I think there are a lot of firms, firms with a whole lot more than $100 to get started, who could benefit from what the book has to say.

Maybe you're miles away from those early days when you were just starting out. Maybe, by some stroke of luck, I'm catching you on Day 1 of your entrepreneurial journey. Wherever you are, I want to devote a chapter to getting scrappy. I want to hearken back to the season of your life when you were just beginning and, once I have you there, I want to put a hunger in your belly to conjure the scrappiness, the tenacity, and the drive, so we can apply it to where you are now.

SEND UP THE TEST BALLOONS

What I love about *The $100 Startup* is its focus. It focuses on people creating their own gigs and opportunities. The book frames it in a pay range of $40k-120K per year. Obviously, with the legal profession we're aiming a good bit higher but there are still some amazing practical tips.

For starters, what are some ways to measure how effective your practices are? What's the minimum amount of data we can swiftly gather to improve our decision-making? I like to talk about test balloons in marketing. These are things like a social media post to see how people respond to a message or a short-term ad buy to check in on the conversion rate of a landing page. It can be as simple as an email to your list designed to drive response. Test balloons can tell us a lot about the market without us having to commit to a direction or fully invest into it.

For example, let's say you've got an idea for the next great referral letter. Or so you think. Before you build out that 12-page letter with a pamphlet (basically betting all on red), do the *$100 Startup* version of it. Put fifty pieces of mail in fifty envelopes with a simple, succinct version of your new message. See how the market responds. Rather than waiting for *perfect* to happen, let the market tell you what it wants. The *$100 Startup* is a fantastic mindset for marketing, because it's addressing things on a small scale, in an elementary fashion.

It is a big focus with law firm owners that I coach. They're looking to go for specific communities and they're thinking about what strategies they can utilize to break into the next economic, cultural or social sphere. The *$100 Startup* is a compelling, energetic framework to get you moving into that community. No matter your work, your first million is built on the back of your first $100,000, which is built on the back of your first $10,000.

Which all comes back to your first $100.

There's a reason the trope of framing your first dollar when you go into business is so pervasive. The first step is always the most important one.

Sending out little test balloons, small and measured half steps, helped me understand what it was the market wanted. What do people actually want? Above all, it keeps you present. If you're really paying attention to people's responses, you're simultaneously acquainting yourself with your community. You learn who you need to be to your community.

When you tap into a community, if your front end is: I'm going to bring this community together. A service oriented front-end drives your back end towards the business aspect: getting referrals out of it.

CONVICTION

Conviction is important. No matter what line of work you get into, a level of passion and interest in what you do is just as essential as discipline, talent and who you know. Sometimes there is just a deep connection with a particular community. I have a coaching client who has a community he has been helping for over a decade. He's really committed to spreading his influence and making a more direct approach with his community. He's coming from a place of service, and it's phenomenal. He'll have an immense amount of success doing it. On the flip side, for some people serving a particular community is a business opportunity. Passion is still essential.

PASSING THE LESSONS DOWN

Entrepreneurship wasn't really a thing growing up in my house. My father was an FBI agent, my mother was a teacher. Solid jobs. Service to others. Specific career paths. There wasn't a model of someone doing something as ridiculous as starting a business. That's not a bad thing. It's a common story. My parents instilled so many important values and traits in me which are the backbone of who I am as a person. And that backbone is what ultimately helped me take the risk to go out on my own. My mom and dad are worth a book of their own in gratitude.

Now, because I have entrepreneurial drive and experience, I want to pass it down to my kiddos. When my girls hit their teenage years, I plan on giving them a copy of *$100 Startup* with a challenge. I want them to find what their version of the *$100 Startup* is. I want them to find something they're passionate about, and I want them to get scrappy. I will fund their initial idea on a very small scale. Then, if they start to see it through, I will help them with more money and support. But they have to show real gumption.

I want my kids to have the courage to make the brave choice of building something new. This means leading the way and giving them the resources (including inspiration) to make it happen.

My challenge for you, at the close of this chapter, is simple. Give someone you love a copy of the *$100 Dollar Startup*. Be the source of inspiration, passion and accountability for someone on their journey. Let's bring a scrappy culture to the marketplace. Let's start building to the next six or seven figures by validating the first $100.

ALCHEMY IN ACTION:

Set up test balloons: Test the small version of your next big idea and get feedback from how the market responds.

Conviction: Cultivate a passion for what you do in addition to building skills, focus and pursuing revenue.

Pass the lessons down: Take what you have learned and find a way to start someone else on their journey.

chapter 16

HEALTHY PROFIT AND GROWTH
WITH MOSHE AMSEL

> *Moshe Amsel* is the founder and CEO of Profit with Law. He is also the host of the Profit with Law Podcast and the Law Firm Growth Summit. He helps law firm owners grow their practice with a focus on creating generational wealth.

WHEN WE BOIL DOWN the art of success in business, it is not just about how good you are at your trade. It has a lot to do with how satisfied your customers are with the experience. I'm going to equate lawyers to another professional service: doctors. What separates good doctors from great ones is how they relate to their patients. How is their bedside manner?

Picture the best cardiologist in the world. Thousands of people a year choose them to have their particular ailments corrected but if those doctors have poor bedside manner, patients will walk away in perfect health but with a less than positive experience. The experience of the client is everything, regardless of the service you offer.

> *And it's not just the experience of serving them.*
> *It's the experience before you serve them.*

Cleo Legal Trends ran a famous test back in 2020. They called over fifteen hundred small firms across the nation to gauge their responsiveness to clients. Not only did the majority of them not answer, but they also failed to return calls after a voicemail was left.

What is it like when somebody calls your firm? What do they experience when the phone is picked up? If it gets picked up. When they walk through the door the first time? The second time? The last time? When their business is finished, and you're parting ways, what is their experience?

I think that is the underlying secret for a healthy law firm. reating an experience that leaves the client raving and sending more business the firm's way. How we do that is not only by examining the client experience, but measuring the vitals of your law firm and creating a roadmap for its growth.

KPIS AND THE CLIENT EXPERIENCE

Law firm owners struggle to understand what they should be measuring. Moreover, they struggle to figure out how to use the measurements they have when creating a strategy to enhance the experience of their clients, increase profit and grow their firm.

The term KPI gets thrown around a lot. It creates a lot of confusion for business owners who know they need to find metrics for success but are uncertain what to measure. Well, you can measure the experience people are having with your business, and I mean tracking what happens at every stage of their journey.

I like to separate KPIs into two types: Firm KPIs and Individual KPIs. A firm KPI is foundational. Everyone, no matter their role, can work towards it. Some examples are client conversions, elevating leads to sales. Individual KPIs are more specialized, based on the employee's role in the firm. They are less about how the firm, as a whole, is serving the customer and more about how the employee knows they are doing a good job.

For example, I'm trying to increase how many clients I'm serving. A firm level KPI could be the percentage of our leads that led to consultations increased over a certain time. The different things employees do while pursuing that goal are individual KPIs.

There might be one person who answers the phone. Someone else is doing an intake call. Someone else is doing the consult. They're all responsible for the collective KPI.

Individual KPIs are less about what you as the manager or owner want to achieve and more about how your employees can measure their own performance. How do they know they are doing a good job? I could put the KPI on the wall and say, "If we hit this metric, then we order a food truck for the quarter. Or everyone gets a bonus. Or an extra vacation day. It drives the team collectively towards a vision.

> **SIDEBAR.** A lot of my clients have questions about KPIs. They struggle to determine what KPIs they should assign to team members.
>
> They struggle trying to find these really individualistic KPIs. Unique to everyone. I challenge them to zoom out a layer. If the idea of KPIs is something you struggle with, try switching your term to metrics. What would be a metric you would track if this were a department you were managing? For example, the number of leads that have been moved to appointments or the number of appointments that became signed clients.
>
> Then, what's the velocity after you've signed a client to the first significant point of action in a personal injury firm? It might be the demand packages sent.
>
> Metric based KPIs level the field and keep everyone fixed on the same goal.

Something I've found helpful is breaking down every step of the client experience, really narrowing it down. If you can identify every step a potential client takes with your firm, it becomes a lot easier to establish concrete, specific and measurable KPIs for your firm in order to hit the mark every time.

What are some of the initial ways the client may interact with you before you ever meet face to face? It might be:

- Clicks on your website

- Views and/or likes on social media

- SEO's and how people are arriving to your website

- Incoming phone calls

After that, the next step might be:

- Answered calls
- Submitted forms
- Leads
- Consultations

Getting specific helps. Getting pedantic helps. Map out every stage of the customer experience and then bullet point the little steps in between. Stretch it out. The more you stretch out the steps, the easier it's going to be to diagnose where your possible points of breakdown are. We can see where we're doing poorly. The numbers can tell us where the problem is, and we can find room to fix it.

For example, let's imagine a scenario where the phone rang one hundred times over the past month and only half of those calls were answered. We've got the symptom, missed phone calls. Now we diagnose the problem. Was the receptionist sick? How much time are they spending on social media? Are they outside on a smoke break every fifteen minutes? First determine whether they are meeting their basic performance function, which in this instance is answering the phone. We want to aspire to go above and beyond, so once we make our diagnosis, we establish an individual KPI. In this example, it could be for every lead that comes in, 80% will become consults. That's a KPI the receptionist is directly responsible for. We have the metrics to reward the KPI being met, and we have information if the receptionist continues to fall short.

However, this formula only gets you the information. What you do after is where your bedside manner becomes essential. What happens next requires emotional intelligence.

EMOTIONAL INTELLIGENCE

We just laid out a formulaic approach to developing a customer experience pipeline, but it still doesn't tell us how to develop the "bedside manner" that's going to address some of those breakdowns of the customer experience.

We've got room to fix problems. We've got the space to elevate the experience. But the metrics we discover are just going to tell us where our problem areas are. They aren't going to fix them.

That's where emotional intelligence comes in.

Perhaps we're seeing a breakdown between the conversion of consults to sales or leads to consultations. We have the numbers to inform us, but now we have to go and diagnose what is causing that problem.

Let's take, for example, an issue that's very common: leads coming in that become consults. A healthy number for that would be 70-80%. High. If they're calling you, they need you. They need a solution, and with the systems you have in place you're able to move the majority of those calls to the next step.

What if those numbers are running low?

Say my phone rings ten times and I'm getting two consults from those calls. That's 20%. They're not taking the next step. It's time to diagnose the problem. How am I failing to set up a conversation to be able to have the next conversation with them.

Where is the breakdown?

It could be anything. Is my consultation free, or is it paid? If it's paid, is that a barrier to entry for potential clients? How am I presenting myself and my firm?

It could be something much more subtle. Am I speaking the same language as them? Is the language of my firm approachable? Inviting? Human?

Find the holes where your firm can benefit from a little emotional intelligence. Some bedside manner. A little more humanity. It's a great opportunity for your marketers to really flex their muscles and establish some branded ways your firm can stand out before your clients ever walk through the door.

The beautiful thing is, once you start monitoring those metrics of the client experience, you can start implementing changes to see improvement. Changes to see growth. Changes to see profit.

LAW FIRM VITALS

A law firm should be making somewhere between 30 and 50% profit on every dollar that comes in.

95% of the law firm owners out there are not making that kind of money.

So where's the drop off? What's the problem?

It all starts with simple, and almost stupid, things like accepting a 20% lead to consult percentage as the cost of doing business. If I'm getting two consults for every ten calls, I could be pouring all my energy, time and resources into marketing and I still won't see growth.

Imagine how much more money I'm going to make if I could get those ten calls to become eight consults, instead of two.

It all starts there. That's the beginning. That's the pipeline coming into the business. Then it continues. The customer is coming through the door, now I have to serve them well.

How can I serve them effectively and efficiently so that I'm moving more clients through with the same number of staff? We can talk about automation and systems and processes, but all of these things are based on the story the numbers are telling me. If I follow the breadcrumbs of those numbers, I can start to unlock the potential of my firm.

Humans have four key vitals: blood pressure, pulse rate, respiratory and blood glucose. When someone is responding to an emergency those are the first things you assess. They tell us how the patient is doing.

Do businesses have something similar? A number you can measure, in an emergency, to determine what kind of health or treatment may be needed?

Absolutely.

The vitals for a business are: **revenue**, **expenses**, and **profit**. Accountants love to dabble and focus on the first two but for myself, I have a profit first mindset. All three are integral at building a clear roadmap to a healthy firm. And a wealthy firm.

The very first thing to look at is how much revenue is coming in, and how much profit is coming from that revenue. That's going to tell an immediate story.

One of my early clients in the legal industry had a $2 million law firm, and she was making $50,000.

Read that a second time.

THEY DON'T TEACH YOU THIS IN LAW SCHOOL

That doesn't compute, right?

My goal for somebody who has a million-dollar firm is to be making $400,000, eight times the amount she was making. With the money she was taking home, she could have gone out and gotten a job at Starbucks and earned more without the hassle that comes from building a multi-million-dollar firm.

So we got to work. We looked at the numbers we had, using the percentages to make it simpler. We took the profit, divided it by the revenue and got 5%. 50,000 divided by 1,000,000. 5%. Next, we figured out the profit margin percentage we wanted to be operating at, 30-50%, anywhere under 30% and there is room for improvement. If I'm operating under 15 or 10%, I'm probably losing sleep at night because it's so razor thin that I'm worried about making payroll.

Those big numbers are the first things I look at when I begin working with a new client. The second is cash flow. Cash flow is very different from profitability. Business owners have a hard time wrapping their head around this. They sit down with their accountant, they see the business had a surplus of $100,000. They see the $50,000 they owe in taxes. They see a bank account sitting at $0. Where's the money going?

It's why expenses become the next integral vital. Determining your cash flow. There are things that you're paying, making payments on, outside of the profit calculation. Things like debt service, loans, credit card payments. Expenses not just from the present but stacked up and incurred over years. Debt service is a big expense that makes it difficult to determine cash flow.

Those big numbers tell a story; learning how to interpret them makes sure it's a good one.

PAY VS PROFIT

There is a big difference between owner pay and profit. Law Firm owners wear a lot of hats and, in the midst of trying to run their business, often try to make them mean the same thing.

Say you go out and buy one hundred shares of stock. By investing, you become a part owner of that company. A shareholder. At the end of the quarter, executive leadership will look at how the company has done. If the company has done well, they'll take a vote and give a percentage of those profits to their shareholders in the form of dividends. You received some of the profit.

There are two things you aren't going to do with those profits.

You aren't going to show up on site, roll up your sleeves and put in a day's work for the profits you've received. You also aren't going to send the check back with a little post-it note telling the company what your dividend check should be spent on to help the company.

Too many owners want to treat their profits as an investor in the company as operational pay for the work they do on a daily basis. It's essential to treat them as two different things. We get into trouble when combining the two. We think of ourselves as just a person, and we mix everything up. When we're short on money, we take our personal funds and we feed it into the firm.

We basically take our profits and give it back. When we have a lot of money, we splurge and spend on the business.

The real problem created by this perspective is twofold. The first is operational. There's no clear understanding of how the business is doing. When we mix pay and profit together, we essentially are giving the business a free employee. We're not trying to make a profit. We're just trying to make a paycheck. It's a dangerous place to operate because it tempts us to make decisions that are unhealthy for the business, because we're wearing two hats.

The second problem is if you ever want to leave. If you wanted to exit your business, to sell it to somebody, it's going to have value because it's profitable. If you never paid yourself or you never looked at your profit as your salary, how are you going to truly know it's value?,

Even if you're not looking to exit, if you start to look at the business from an investor perspective, it puts a totally different spin on where you are. It's important to have that delineation, and not just to have it, but to have a process where we're paying ourselves two different ways. One is our paycheck, our owners pay, and the other is the profit.

PROFIT FIRST

In the high-profit, high growth formula for a law firm we are not far off from private equity entering into the conversation. In the state of Arizona you can own a law firm without being a practicing attorney. It's a bit of a sandbox project and you need approval by the state but it's already there and in practice, and I can foresee the idea catching on.

The way I see it, there are two ways to start a business. The first is to possess a specific skill set and establish a business around that skill set. That means opening the doors as the practitioner, building the business up, and eventually expanding by hiring other practitioners to provide the same service within the business.

The other way is to recognize a market for specific services and hiring individuals with a certain skill set, facilitating all the other aspects of the business and collecting the profit.

If we look at anybody who has built a business with multiple employees working for them, they either were not the primary practitioner or they had a partner that wasn't a practitioner to handle things like accounting, marketing, payroll etc. . They had the realization early on that if they were the practitioner, they were holding themselves back.

If I were to open a law firm in Arizona, who would be the first person I have to hire? I'm not an attorney. How do I provide legal services without an attorney? Before I hire a receptionist, a virtual assistant, or a receptionist I need an attorney. I have to be able to provide the service my business is built around.

I'm sure the idea of hiring additional staff might sound scary for a solo firm owner whose used to wearing all of the hats. The truth is, if you view your firm as a job then the expenses of additional staff will be scary. However, if you view it as an investment then that division of labor will get you to that place of exponential success so much faster.

The road to success may be a long one no matter what, but you control the velocity at which you travel it.

WHEN TO HIRE STAFF

You're never going to be ready to hire someone else.

Never.

There is never a juncture in your business career that you will say,

"I have enough money in my business that I can go hire the next person."

If you remove the fear, and hesitation, how do you know when you're ready? And who do you look at bringing on first?

If you approach it as an investor, the very first thing you would do is hire an attorney. Then the very next thing you do is invest in ways to fill that attorney's plate with clients. Within 90 days, you would have a $400K-500K annual revenue stream that's only costing you $100K-200K depending on your attorney's pay and marketing costs.

I oversimplified it, but that's really what we're talking about. The business of law is the business of selling people's time, and the people are your inventory. The more people in your inventory, the more you can produce. It may be practical to wait until the money is there to employ someone, but the profit-minded investment is in hiring someone to help generate the money to afford them.

It's less about carrying an entire annual salary and more about carrying them for the first 90 days. Within that time they can start improving the top line, which will ultimately pay for their salary and then rapidly pay for the business. Ten to twelve weeks of salary. Can you get your hands on $20,000, yes or no? If you could, go hire yourself an attorney.

The way that I deal with this with my clients is I ask them where they want to go. Where do they want to be in twelve months? Do they want a million-dollar revenue firm? Two million? Once we determine that we paint a picture.

How many attorneys do we need to make a million dollars? How many paralegals?

What does this look like?

How many clients am I serving?

We get those numbers, and they become our firm KPIs and, hopefully, we use those metrics to reach our end result. Once you have an attorney, I often advise finding an inexpensive overseas virtual assistant. Start getting the crazy simple things off your plate. Find someone to take care of collection and billing. When it's covered, find someone to answer emails and talk to clients. Hand it all off to somebody. Then, take the time you just unlocked and go find yourself an attorney.

ALCHEMY IN ACTION:

Examine the client experience: Curate the experience your clients have, from before the first phone call to the last bill being paid.

KPIs: Establish firm and individual KPIs to measure how your team is going above and beyond.

Emotional intelligence: Develop a strong bedside manner. Meet the client where they are.

Law firm vitals: Take regular metrics of your firm's health. Let the numbers tell their story

Pay vs. profit: Understand the difference of operational pay and investor profit.

Profit first: Invest in the direction of growth.

Don't shy away from hiring: Hire people for the business you want.

chapter 17

PRINCIPLED LEADERSHIP
WITH BRANDON OSTERBIND

Brandon Osterbind is a Personal Injury Lawyer based out of Virginia. Over the years he's been recognized repeatedly for his hard work in a variety of mediums. He was named Rising Star by Virginia Super Lawyers Magazine every year since 2016. He was named part of the Top 40 under 40 by the American Association of Legal Advocates. He has argued, and won, twice in the Supreme Court of Virginia and he was designated one of the top 100 Civil Plaintiff's Lawyers in Virginia by the National Trial Lawyers

THERE ARE SO MANY UPS and downs in the day-to-day practice of the law. I don't think there's anything to prepare you for it, save for building up the muscles from going through it. One day you get your client a million-dollar settlement and you're on the top of your game. The next day you go to trial, contributory negligence, a defense verdict, and you're back on the bottom again.

There are certain things in the profession that are impossible to prepare for, which is so incongruous with the world law school tries to prepare you for. It's been a minute since I was in law school, but *preparedness* was drilled into me with a diamond level intensity, and no one ever had the good grace to tell me the world sometimes leaves you unprepared.

I remember a criminal law professor I had. He would call on students at random to stand up and give their answers and the consequences, at least for law school; if you were unprepared it was sink or swim. He would kick you out of class. A day came when he called my name. I did the reading. I thought I was prepared. He hit me with question after question. I had no idea what he was talking about. I became flustered. Finally, he moved on from me.

Later that day I got an email from him:

> **Mr. Osterbind. You were dangerously close to being unprepared today...**

I had come dangerously close to getting kicked out of his class. It happens more often than you think in Law School, a legion of professors ready to deal out consequences for lack of preparedness. You think to yourself, "If I can get through these classes, this isn't going to happen to me in real life. I'll be prepared for anything coming my way. I'll always be prepared."

It's simply not the case.

Everyday there are things vying for my attention. There are an abundance of cases I'm working on. Judges demand a certain quality of work. There are financial ups and downs, an economic roller coaster with no seat belts or height restrictions. One month you might make six figures, the next you're limping at $6,000. And no one tells you about it. No one tells you just how unprepared you will be for those peaks and valleys, when you take a leadership role with a law firm.

CONTROL AND COMMUNICATION

When we're in a season of winning, it's easy to feel on top of the world. It's easier to face those occasional losses with resolve and resilience. The same resolve and resilience can be a scant resource when we hit those valleys. In those seasons, if you zoom out and try to shoulder the emotional load of everything around you, it can really weigh on you. The first piece of advice I have is to handle what's directly in front of you. Work one case at a time. Send one email at a time. Take it one day at a time.

Do the next right thing. Keep the focus on what you can directly control about your circumstances to climb uphill to your next mountain. Ask yourself, "What's missing from my firm's practices to make this simpler?" Look for the actions you take to alleviate the emotional or financial strain of those hills and valleys and build it into a practice. A great example of this is effective communication.

One of the things lawyers don't do very well is communicate frequently, and effectively, with clients. At our firm, we've developed a method of clear communication I'm proud of. We lay the groundwork from the moment the client walks through the door. We explain how we'll communicate with them throughout the course of their case. We use a case management system with a client portal, notifying the client every time there's action on their end or an event they need to attend.

They have options for text, email and messages directly in the system. They see every document pertaining to their case as it comes in, and every one going out. The communication is transparent, inclusive, and instantaneous.

It's natural to want to have a buffer between what you see and what the clients see. It's understandable to want to have the opportunity to spare them from unwanted news.

The way I see it, though, **it's not our case. It's the client's case.**

They have a greater right to know about what's going on in their case than I do. Who am I to withhold information from them and to give it to them on my terms? It's their case. I try to put the ego aside and with clear and open communication build trust with the client. Doing so gets the client in our corner so when the trial gets pushed back, when a complication arises, or bad news comes down the pipe, there is a clear understanding I am on their side and doing what is in my control to get them the best outcome.

The communication we developed does more than create trust with our clients, it creates accountability. Those same two qualities play a vital role in how I manage my team to ensure we all navigate uncertainty with equal resolve and resiliency. This is especially true when someone misses the mark.

There is a great quote from Dan Coyle's *Culture Code:* **"The Road to success is paved with mistakes well handled."** There has to be open communication about mistakes. It's part of the culture of our firm. Everyone makes mistakes, but not everyone handles them equally.

How do you handle the mistake? Do you cover it up? Gloss over it? Lie? Obviously, there are wrong ways to handle mistakes.

Do you come to me when you make a mistake so we can fix it? Do you own it? Do you grow? We should be able to communicate about our successes but it shouldn't stop there. We should also communicate the things we don't necessarily do well. We should communicate where we need help, or room to grow. It's the only way we get better, and it's the only way mistakes will get fixed.

LEADERSHIP AND DELEGATION

When you've been running your own firm for any length of time, delegation can be hard. You have a deeply personal investment in your business. It takes a deep amount of trust to hand the reins of control over to someone else.

When I bring someone on, I don't just give them my trust. I give them the responsibility of doing the work the way I want it done. When I was first expanding my firm, I did all of the onboarding myself. I would sit down and go through policies, procedures, the to-do's and not-to-do's. While it wasn't the best use of my time as an attorney, taking the time to personally invest that level of responsibility to someone paid off. The people I took time to mold now have a degree of supervisory authority. They handle the training, and they do it how I want it done, because they went through the same training themselves.

Once you get the right people in place, meet with them regularly. Keep apprised of what's been happening, what's happening, and what's about to happen. Develop a rhythm to your meetings. Our leadership team is composed of my lead paralegal, my associate attorney and my wife who is also an attorney at the practice. Over time we've developed our own EOS and have a set-in-stone time, every week, to meet for ninety minutes. We discuss everything from issues we're having, to priorities, limitations and, most importantly, what direction we're going in.

We try to live the culture of our firm, within the small group, then allow it to expand to the larger firm as a whole. Another weekly meeting I keep on the books is with my lead paralegal. They have their direct reports bring them up to speed and, at our weekly meeting, we figure out where we should be and what happens next. Communication is simultaneous from the top down, and the bottom up. A lot of good leadership comes from clarity, awareness and communication.

NAVIGATE WITH CORE VALUES

Your core values should be at the center of everything you do. They should influence your hiring, who you are with clients and the decisions you make. Core values aren't who you want to be, or who you're aspiring to be in ten years. They directly reflect who you are, now, in this moment.

Five or so years ago, we picked out seven or eight "core values" and we put them up on our website. They were outward facing. I couldn't tell you what they were, we just thought it was important to list them. We listed them, but we weren't living them.

So we took a full day. We put all other things on hold, and we figured it out. We threw out the seven or eight on our website and we took time to really see one another. We shared the things we saw in our colleagues and people we associate with. We highlighted the qualities we wanted to emulate. We distilled the lengthy list into just three values: **courageous, driven, invested**.

They were simple. They were easy to remember. Most importantly, they were true.

If you're not courageous, driven and invested, we don't have a place for you with our firm. After we defined those values, we broke them into subcategories.

What does it mean to be invested? We have to be invested in each other. I have to be invested in your success, and you have to do likewise. We have to be invested in the cases and clients we work with. We have to be invested in our community.

Figure out the ways you can take your values and turn them into action.

Core values also give you a shared language to lift your colleagues up. Remember, they aren't something you aspire to. They're who you already are. A few months back we had one of our monthly 'lunch and learns', a monthly opportunity for us to catch up as a team and develop together. Our associate attorney was leading the lunch and, at the end, she went around the table and identified an example of how each person exhibited our values in the last thirty days. It was pretty emotional. When people hear how something they did made a difference, lived up to a clearly-defined higher ideal, it sticks with them. It lights them up.

Our core values empower and shape our decision making. From the head of the firm looking ahead to the next year, to a receptionist looking to the next phone call, core values ensure you come from a place of principle rather than comfort or self-interest.

PRINCIPLED LEADERSHIP

Faith plays a huge role in my life. I've been a Christian since I was seven years old. I was brought up in faith and it's a huge part of my story. It has directed who I am and still drives who I want to be. When situations strike me as uncomfortable, I feel compelled to do the right thing with no gray area in between.

There are things in this world society or culture push on us. They want you to think, speak, shop and spend a certain way. I can't follow that. My response is an unyielding "no". I will never follow the crowd if I know the crowd is wrong. There's got to be some extra systemic validator to everything that happens. Everywhere you turn there is someone else giving you their version of the truth but, to me, there is only one truth. There is an external truth outside of all of us and we don't get to decide what it is. We have to discover what truth is, and it takes hard work.

You have to determine where the truth is, what it is and what it means for your life. Now we're getting really deep because I don't think that the truth is what you say it is because you say it, or because you think it, or because you believe it and feel it. There is one truth. There is an external truth outside of all of us, and we don't get to decide what it is. We have to find out what it is. We have to discover what that truth is.

I'm miles away from the kid in Law School who thought things would be clearer after the BAR. Life stacks on itself and, outside of professional obligations, there is a life's worth of personal responsibility to reconcile with every day. A life's worth, and it moves so quickly. I have four beautiful kids, an incredible wife, and an active life at church. Sometimes I feel like a glorified taxi driver. Every day I blink and it feels like another year has passed.

It moves so quickly. My wife and I try to stay mindful, as hard as some days are, there will come a day really soon where we'll look back and miss it. We try to keep a mindset of gratitude and stay intentional about doing things to have a maximum impact on our kids. We get to pass down these principles to inform their lives. It's a huge responsibility. It's an even greater privilege.

Principles and Values are what has informed me as a leader. Communication is how I choose to lead. The responsibility and privilege I feel, in the midst of those hills and valleys impossible to fully prepare for, is by far the greatest reward.

ALCHEMY IN ACTION:

Control and communication: Do the next right thing. Focus on what is in your control. Keep communication of what you can and can't control open.

Delegation: Take the steps necessary to invest trust in others to fulfill roles aligned with your values

Navigate with core values: determine what currently defines you. Develop a shared language with your team around them to highlight work aligning with those values

Principled leadership: Stand for what you believe in and let it dictate how you move through the world.

chapter 18

THE COACHING PYRAMID
– CHARLEY

THERE ARE CERTAIN, fundamental, principles I bring to the table with all of my coaching clients. One of them is a basic triangle I use to get a sense of where potential problems are, and what work needs to be done to solve them. The triangle is formed by three words that each operate as a leg propping up the law-firm stool. Their words are marketing, operations, and finance. Each definition means a little more than the word itself.

For example, **marketing** is really marketing and sales. We put both of those in the same bucket. Attraction and conversion.

Operations is all of the legal operations that you have across different practice areas along with your administrative needs. To simplify it, operations is about systems and people.

Finance encompasses more than just monitoring money. It's building financial controls, setting up new metrics, and holding departments accountable to a budget. It's probably the hardest part to master because most law firm owners just want to know the general status of the money. Is there any in the bank? Will that cover the next couple of months? Great. We're all good.

These three legs weave into one another. Operations includes people who handle the intake process and selling, so it bleeds into marketing. Marketing involves advertising, which means spending money, so finance needs to get involved. Finance involves people which weave into operations. It's all interconnected and sometimes confusing, but I'll do my best to make sense of it for you.

THE TRIANGLE

I would love for you to draw a simple triangle with marketing at the top. From the top, draw an arrow down and to the right pointing to the bottom foundation: operations. Take a hard left turn and draw an arrow pointing to the other foundation: finance. Next, bring it home by drawing an arrow to the top of the pyramid back to marketing.

There's a reason for this specific order. I describe it best like this: The job of marketing is to go and get clients for the firm. By getting a ton of clients and being really great at their job, marketing creates problems for operations. Operations then has to actually handle the work, be properly staffed, create the systems in order to accomplish the work marketing has brought in. To do that there have to be investments made into operations, which puts us right back to finance. Finance is then going to look to marketing and sales to get more clients and a better profit margin, creating more work for marketing.

One of the reasons I like using this triangle is it shows the relationship between parts of the practice that could otherwise feel siloed. If I am working with a client, and they've been doing their marketing well, chances are they're creating issues for operations. More cases means a need for more people and better systems. Now we need to go into operations and solve those problems. We make improvements in one area which upset the balance somewhere else, so we improve that and the cycle continues.

As we say in another chapter, **where focus goes energy flows** Putting considerable focus on one element of the triangle at a time is really beneficial, especially early on. As the firm matures and grows, you will have team members who work on improvements across the entire firm. Your job morphs into making sure everyone is still heading in the same direction. Each department needs to work toward a collective vision, not just what pops into the mind of the department head that day.

As we put our focus on marketing and the cases start to pile up, we turn our attention to operations. In operations, systemize. We study the skillsets we're missing. We find the staff to fill vacancies. We put our maximum focus and force into succeeding operationally. It's often a lot easier to make improvements to operations when your marketing is in place to generate cases and revenue. Suddenly, you need to hire people to manage your new workload. Building systems become less of a financial burden, and it's time to turn your energy to finances. You're looking at increased revenue. It's time to solidify profit margins and bring brand new efficiencies into practice. We focus on the data.

The other part of finance is establishing some level of data tracking. It's not that data doesn't play a role in other places, but it's the data from finance that informs the other tiers of the triangle. Take the time to find the data set that is actually valuable and worth tracking. Find the data that will allow your marketing to ratchet up. Every cycle matters. Deliberate focus on each creates a cycle of upward inertia.

KEEP IT SIMPLE

The primary purpose of this tool is to simplify your workflow. It's meant to provide clarity and help streamline your focus as you guide your ship and crew on the entrepreneurial seas.

Often, a maxim in entrepreneurship is "Why make something easier on yourself when you can make it ten times more complicated" and I've seen it many times with this model. Don't try to tackle everything, with all of them, all at once. Rather, do enough with one then turn your attention to the next.

The most common thing I see happening when a client begins working with the triangle is they'll try to customize it, and in doing so, complicate it. A firm will either go from marketing to operations and then back to marketing, or a firm will go marketing straight to finance completely bypassing operations.

In the spirit of real entrepreneurship there's a lot of growth that can happen by just finding the ways the triangle occurs naturally in the practice. Most firms are obsessive about the trajectory of operations into finance. They are either extremely referral heavy or they have stalled out and can't find the next level of growth. Both are missing one of the core, growth oriented, parts of this triangle. The power of this model is its simplicity. Keep. It. Simple.

I could take this model and put it into any business and produce results with it. It has a broad application, due to its simplicity.

Marketing creates problems for operations. Operations creates problems for finance. Finance creates new problems for marketing. We keep repeating this, over and over. When I'm in rhythm with a client, we're going to see a transition to the next area of focus usually every six months. Other clients will be on a three-month quarterly cycle. The timelines vary, but it is important to stick to them.

TIMELINES OF TRANSITION

When it comes to marketing, for example, you may put a new strategy into play and not see the results for 45-90 days. In some cases with long term strategies, like bigger referrals through newsletters and search engine optimization, it could take 6-12 months before you see results and are ready to transition to operations.

If you find yourself constantly mired in one space, and not turning your attention to the other, your firm will languish. You will atrophy certain parts of the practice. A better term for it might be habituate. Certain things will become habit, which will entropy into the culture, which will make it harder to enforce the flexibility needed to work the pyramid.

If you are never tinkering with each of these spaces within a twelve-month period, you risk your staff getting stuck in re-dundancy. They'll lose the flexibility to easily transition to the next space. If you've been focusing exclusively on marketing for six months, take some time to deviate. Ask for improvements on systems. Figure out your staffing needs. Let that naturally lead you to finance so you can learn your numbers. Familiarizing yourself with your numbers, frequently and deliberately, will help keep consistent profit margins and allow for higher predictability on a quarter-to-quarter basis.

FINANCIAL RHYTHM

Without good financial rhythms we can't invest in new marketing. We can't invest in new systems. We can't bring on new people.

When I talk about the numbers, I am talking how much money you collect, not how much your cases are worth overall. That's the point of interest. You're a million-dollar firm when you cover a million dollars in fees, not when you have a million dollars in settlements or verdicts.

By better understanding our numbers we have the opportunity to reinvest in the practice. We can truly treat it like a business. Which is why finance cycles back into marketing. The question I have now is:

Where are you on the triangle?

Where do you think you are being pulled the most? What is coming next for you? By knowing where you are, and where you are going, you can anticipate your readiness to focus on the next space. You can at least decide when you're ready to focus on that space.

This is the fundamental difficulty of running any business. It's not easy to do this. I will give a final recommendation here as we wrap up this chapter. As you move through the triangle, build on what you've accomplished by leaving something behind.

Leave behind a new asset, a new system, or a new person. It needs to be something that can ultimately be handed off, passed down , or delegated to another individual. Whatever you do as you move forward, try and set up something that keeps working long after you have moved on to the next stage in your practice. Leave something behind that is unique to you.

One of the big things that will eventually happen as you scale, if you're growing a larger law firm, is you will leave behind valuable people to grow each one of those spaces for you. You will be able to put less effort into growing. You can put your energy into being a leader. The work will begin to stack on itself until, one day, you build something which, like the pyramids themselves, stand the test of time.

ALCHEMY IN ACTION:

Work the pyramid: Deliberately alternate between marketing, operations and finance.

Keep it simple: Focus on one area at a time, moving linearly from one focus to the next.

Stay on timelines: Don't linger too long on one area and risk building bad habits.

Leave something behind: Each time you move on, leave something behind to ensure your systems can succeed and your business can grow.

chapter 19

CONNECTING
PEOPLE WITH STORIES
WITH ANDREW AYERS

*Before he started his own law firm, **Andrew Ayers** worked for a few different law firms in New York City. He still co-counsels most of them to this day. Working with some exceptional lawyers taught Andrew the importance of personal relationships in the legal profession, and working for a family lawyer taught him the pitfalls of ignoring those relationships. It was a lesson in what not to do when trying to run a law firm.*

When it came time to start his own law firm, those experiences helped Andrew understand the challenges and opportunities which confront business owners at all stages of their entrepreneurial journeys. Andrew was amazed at the creative and innovative businesses being launched, and even more impressed by the people behind those businesses. Working with those amazing people, Andrew quickly learned that the heart of a small business is constantly adapting to the changing markets we all operate in.

> *Over the past 20+ years, Andrew's business has evolved to work with small businesses and the innovating people who run them. Whether it's working on a lawsuit for the business or creating estate planning for their family, he always strives to remember that the law is a deeply personal profession.*
>
> *Andrew is a master at shaping a Law Firm around what he's passionate about, and demonstrating the work he does through marketing. He tries to foster a strong relationship with his clients by being consistent, being authentic and being connected.*

THE MOST SUCCESSFUL LAWYERS I've worked with recognize the point where their knowledge stops, and there's someone else who knows more than they do. Rather than waste their energy trying to reinvent the wheel, they're open and willing to find someone to help guide them towards a solution. The best attorneys embrace this mindset.

When I was starting out, I felt reluctant to ask for help when I needed it. I was nervous about what the more senior attorneys and judges would think if I came to them with that level of vulnerability. Vulnerability is not instilled into you in Law School. What I discovered, happily and to my surprise over the years, is asking for help actually got me further. Those senior attorneys and judges weren't only willing to talk, they were happy to help.

THE PEOPLE BEHIND THE PROFESSION

When I was starting out, I was scared to ask questions. I was thrown right into family law as a young associate in New York

City. I was in the deep end of a motion hearing my first week. I had a boss who was too busy, a lot of stress and so many questions I needed answers to. I needed help.

By a sheer stroke of luck, I ran into a friend on my way to the hearing who knew the judge who would be presiding. He gave me advice about what I should do, how to navigate, and above all reminded me of something I try to hold onto in my work.

Behind all of the titles and accomplishments, the professionals we work with are just people. When you have the opportunity, **meet the people behind the profession**.

I started learning to reach out. I think part of what broke down the wall for me was finding ways to connect with lawyers outside of the courtroom. One way I do this is tennis. I play a couple of times a week. I have my core group I play with. A few are lawyers. Two are retired judges. When we get together, we set the law aside and we just play. We connect on a personal level, and it breaks down barriers which could otherwise arise.

It's easy to assume the judge sitting on the bench, or the CEO on the top floor, wouldn't have the time or energy for you. The fact is they won't unless you ask. When you ask, you might be surprised to find the time they're willing to give you.

Years ago when I was admitted to the US Supreme Court, Justice Alito and Justice Ginsburg came and spoke to my group. I was struck with how down to earth they were. They were personable, they were social, they were <u>human</u>. It's so easy to lose sight of our shared humanity. We live in a world of status, and social hierarchy. At the end of the day, we're all just people. We put our pants on one leg at a time. We all commute home. We all fall asleep with hopes of having better days ahead than bad. There is a common ground to the human experience which, if you can bring it to your work, can help you connect with people.

The law is an incredibly intimidating profession. It is also a deeply personal profession. We deal with people. Breaking down barriers, and connecting with people, is a huge way I've overcome the fear and intimidation which comes with practicing law.

Becoming a lawyer can be incredibly isolating. You can end up walking a very lonely road. You're taught in law school to chase being the top of your class. It's drilled into you to go after the best jobs, doing whatever it takes to get there, and discovering there's no one else around you. I certainly struggled with a lot of personal demons on my own journey. It can be lonely, but it doesn't have to be.

Look long enough, and you'll find there are so many other people who are just as lonely as you, who are anxious for connection. There are people who want to talk and want to help. There is so much connective tissue between people, it just takes the courage to ask. Go deeper than asking about the weather. Take time to get to know people.

Allow yourself to be known. Share your passions. Ask about theirs. Figure out how you can help one another on your journeys. It can make the road less lonely and accelerate where you want to go along the road.

FIND THE NEXT STEP

If loneliness is the biggest emotional obstacle you'll have to face, the biggest professional one is inertia. Getting comfortable, and stagnant, will put miles between you and your goals. If you want to work for yourself and be your own boss, you can't be static.

I remember years ago seeing attorneys in court, and it struck me just how glazed over they seemed. They were in the same court room, day after day, getting adjournment after adjournment. They were living the same day, over and over again. It really left an impression on me and I realized early in my career I wanted more than routine and repetition. I had a new daughter at home, my wife and I both wanted more, and I felt afraid the work I was doing was becoming incongruous with the life I wanted to have and the time I wanted to spend with my new family.

I didn't want to do what I was doing, but I was unclear on the next step. I had several clients at the time who were business owners, and I found myself interested in what they had to say. I found them engaging. Hearing them talk about their business and finding the next steps gave me a frame of mind I've applied to my own career.

When faced with uncertainty, find the next step.

I began to apply it to my career, taking things one step at a time. We moved from Brooklyn to New Jersey, then from New Jersey to Minnesota. I went from working in a firm with a depressing office culture to working for myself and loving every minute of it. **You don't have to know the destination, you just need to know where to put your foot down next.**

Just keep moving and find what the next opportunity is. Above all, make sure the next step excites you. Pick what ignites your passion. The great thing about law is there is a wide array of ways to pursue your trade. If something is engaging to you, build your business model around it. I started my business model with the question,

"Is this going to engage me?" There have been certain areas of practice and, after reflection, I've decided not to touch. They just don't hold my interest. I'm not passionate about it.

Over the years I've met a lot of attorneys who are doing the work just to collect a paycheck. They're miserable in court. They're doing a job they hate, and it bleeds over into how they relate to their clients, to their colleagues and to themselves. It's not who I want to be. When you see attorneys with an authentic and honest passion for their work and their clients, it's contagious.

Whenever you're at a crossroads trying to find the next step, ask what's going to keep you engaged.

CONSISTENCY BUILDS CONFIDENCE

Nobody graduates from law school, business school, or any school, and has the perfect career. You're going to make mistakes along the way, and you just have to realize they're inevitable. You'll live. Mistakes aren't fatal, and you can learn and grow from them. If you have a strong network of people to talk to, you can minimize those mistakes and the effect they have on your life. I've never been someone overflowing with confidence. It's grown over the years as I've made connections and engaged in work that I am passionate about, but it's taken time.

Starting out, I struggled with imposter syndrome. I think it's common among new lawyers. I'd find myself in these big groups of experienced people and think, "I don't belong here." I hyper fixated on what they seemed to have, which I lacked. They had more money, more confidence, more charisma. More. More. More. In focusing on what I perceived they had, I held myself back.

I'll circle back to what I said in the beginning of the chapter. When you meet someone who has qualities you admire, join their circle. Ask them questions. Learn their work practices. Acquire new tools. Confidence comes with time. Confidence without skill is just ego. True confidence comes from consistent practice. Confidence comes from fully embracing who you are.

Some clients hire me for the degrees hanging on my wall. I like to think more clients hire me for *The Mandalorian* poster they see in the background of my Youtube videos, or the antique grandfather clock sitting on my desk. People don't want to hire your law degree or your law firm letterhead. They want to hire you. It also helps bridge the confidence gap. Some people may be smarter, or have better credentials, but there is only one you. No one knows your story better than you do.

TELLING STORIES FOR WIDER AUDIENCES

Whether we like it or not, social media is the pathway to direct traffic to your business. It provides an incredible opportunity not only to get your brand out there, but add the right amount of personality to make you stand out from the thousands of other law firms trying to do the same thing. A number of years ago, I started a YouTube channel for my firm, as a way to generate leads and also get information into present and future clients' hands. When I started, I could do about two to three minutes at a time, making sure I never strayed too far from the careful notes I took to stay on message. These days, it's all off the cuff, and I find myself striving more and more for brevity instead of struggling to keep the video going. I went from trying to impart information to telling stories. That's what good social media is all about. **Tell a story so people want to know more and learn it from you.** It's important to remember, anytime you embark on something like this, you aren't going to get where you want to be overnight. It takes years to cultivate a following and develop your voice.

I can distill my social media strategy into three action items: *Be consistent*, *be authentic*, and *be connecte*d.

-Be Consistent

The first thing I do, which I learned years ago, is to block plan my week. I plan it all out on Sunday morning, without fail. No excuses. There are certain bricks of time on my calendar which are going to be there, no matter what. I have to make time for it. My videos are a part of it. Once a month, I shoot between eight to ten videos, nearly a month's worth of content which I can then schedule to go out in ways that align with my social strategy. Looking back, it's really great to see how much more comfortable and confident I am now than when I started. It affirms so much of what I've come to believe about confidence. If you put in the work, you will get better. At the start, you don't need to be totally confident. You just need to be open to getting better and growing. Consistency yields capability, and capability yields confidence.

-Be Authentic

An overarching thing is to make sure it's me. You'll never present better when you're presenting as yourself. I remember when I did my very first videos, a couple of years ago. I went upstairs into this huge conference room here in our building. I set up a tripod. I had my tie. I was horribly formal. It wasn't me. It's still on my channel. I've made a promise to myself to never take it down, because I enjoy going back and seeing where I started. When I present now, I talk to the camera the same way I would speak to a client. I sit at my desk and, above all, I focus on being authentically myself. It's a small adjustment which has made a huge difference.

A frequent bit of feedback I love getting from my clients is, when they call me, they say they can clearly picture my face. Having watched my videos, they can visualize my mannerisms and expressions. They have a mental picture of me in their mind. I see it as a huge win, and proof in the conclusion that people who seek legal representation really value feeling a connection with the person over their expertise.

-Be Connected

I focus more on nurturing the connections I have than I do bringing in new people. I think it's important. My channel has hit over 1,000 subscribers, which for a legal based channel is no easy feat. In addition to the subscribers on my channel, I have my email list. We do book giveaways several times a year. Books are a huge part of my practice. Sometimes it's cookbooks, or a book I'm currently reading. One Halloween I gave away a children's book. I nurture the people we're associated with. I send regular emails, newsletters and birthday cards.

There are a lot of times when people don't remember who their lawyers was. Staying connected with them is a way to remind them, "Hey, I'm here to help." Nurturing your clients and staying connected with them doesn't need to be complicated. On the contrary, I've had far more success by just **keeping it simple**.

I have a standard format for all of my emails. I divided them into three different sections. The first section is usually a legal topic I think people on my list would find engaging. Section two is a charity piece. I'll direct traffic to a charity on any variety of causes, usually associated with times of the year where organizations are trying to raise awareness about one cause or another. The third piece is about the latest content on my YouTube channel.

It doesn't need to be really involved, it just needs to be consistent and connect people to various avenues of your work. This type of work isn't scalable, it's just good practice.

CONNECTING PEOPLE TO THEIR STORIES

Stories are powerful things. They do so much more than convey simple information, and simple lessons. They empathetically connect people to circumstances otherwise outside themselves.

They put people in one another's shoes. I love using storytelling, both for my YouTube channel and in my copywriting. What I try to do first, when I want to use an experience from my legal work, is look at my best clients and figure out where they were in their process. What was their struggle? What was their story? Their names aren't important.

Bob and Jane Smith came to me and signed a will.

Bob and Jane had a couple of kids who, as they got older, blessed them with grandchildren.
Bob and Jane knew they had some changes they wanted to make, to make sure they left a legacy behind for the people who mattered most to them.

You tell the story well. You tell the story simply. Suddenly, to a person listening, they're thinking of their neighbor or their grandparents when they visualize Bob and Jane. Maybe they even see themselves in the story.

People's connection to the stories and studying the direct response from them infuses a massive human element to a profession which often lacks it. The law can be very opaque. No body wants to read a letter saying,

You need an estate plan. Here are five documents you need. Sign here. Give me your money.

NO-BODY LIKES A LAWYER, EVERYONE NEEDS ONE

People don't want legalese. People want stories.

They want Bob and Jane. They want emotions. This might be a radical opinion, especially in a book about legal marketing, but *no-body likes lawyers.*

Maybe a more accurate statement is *no-body wants a lawyer, but everyone at some point in their lives will need a lawyer.*

When someone comes to talk to me about a will, it's not a happy place to be. They don't want to think about what happens when they die. They're there to talk about business. If you can add a bit of humanity to the process, it can ease what could otherwise be something sterile, uncomfortable and unpleasant.

Social Media and marketing are about connecting. We have a huge opportunity as lawyers to find people across the various networks and bring them onto your own personal network you can cultivate. The most effective social media, though, are your referrals. It's in the people you know, and the personal connections you've made. The ability to connect with people isn't scalable, it's just something you have to get better at and incorporate into your work. It's why those earliest lessons of asking for help, and asking questions, are still so prevalent in the work I do today.

Take time to learn people's birthdays. Invest in their interests. Figure out how to incorporate it into your business and, above all, **take the time to listen.**

The most valuable thing you can give to people is your time. I wouldn't be where I am today if it weren't for the people who took time out of their weeks to talk to me, answer my questions and invest in what was important to me. For those beginning their journeys, have the confidence to ask for the time. For those who have arrived in a place where they feel energized and excited about the work they do, give the gift of listening. No matter what end of the road you're on, both have the enormous potential for learning. A lot of learning can happen when you put down the titles and just share a story.

ALCHEMY IN ACTION:

Step beyond the title: Meet the person behind the profession.

Do the next right thing: When faced with uncertainty, find the next step.

Consistently build confidence: Let confidence come as a result of practice and mastering skills

Tell a good story: Utilize storytelling to draw people in, and learn more.

chapter 20

THE GUT-CHECK MOMENT
– CHARLEY

I WANT TO TALK about the band Chumbawumba.

Stop!

I'm kidding!

Please, don't shut the book.

I just want to talk about that one song. Really the only song they're known for. You know it:

> *"I get knocked down. But I get up again.*
> *You're never gonna keep me down"*

There's a reason those lyrics stick out nearly thirty years after the single dropped. It's an anthem for the underdog. It commands a sense of excellence in the face of adversity. It leaves room to celebrate the win. It gives the listener teeth if they're facing a loss. That's why it sticks out to me and why it's worth this little intermission chapter.

Winning is highly reinforcing. It's addictive. We get a little kick of dopamine with every victory, leaving us scrambling to capture the feeling we had the first time we won. A lot of marketing is built on it. Gambling is constructed around it. Life, itself, is a series of highs and lows. The view from the top is always sweetest. But what happens when you come down from that winning streak? What about when you come down from that mountain to find yourself back in the trench?

LEAN INTO THE RESISTANCE

Your first time up to the plate was a home run.
You're on a roll. Next comes a double. A triple. The stadium thunders. Fans are cheering. Your team couldn't look prouder. The bases are loaded and, once more, you step up to the plate with a heap of expectation and a whole lot to live up to.

Suddenly you get the yips. Your wrist locks up. Your streak is over when it counts the most and your luck suddenly seems behind you. After a long run of success, things seem to turn on you. Maybe a sports metaphor doesn't suit you. Maybe it's a dud of a social media post after several pieces of high-performing content. Maybe you're suddenly getting less engagements from your email.

Sometimes we get this really early success, often because we have something to say or the energy to accomplish what we set out to achieve but then we plateau. Then we meet with resistance and when we do, that's when we get to lean in and figure out who we have to be going forward.

Who am I when the first batch of ideas or the first bit of excitement has waned. What am I going to put out there?

How do I continue to play the game?

In that gut-check moment you meet resistance you have two choices. You can dedicate yourself to becoming better than the obstacles in front of you, or you can decide you're in the wrong arena and leave to pursue the right one. That second option might sound a lot like quitting, but I like to think of it more like developing efficiency with your talents. You're stepping away from one strategy to try another. You're zooming out. You're testing and experimenting how to better utilize your skills.

When you hit those moments of resistance ask yourself, "Do I just need to figure out how to press through? Can this obstacle be solved with my current strategy if I just put in the work?" If no amount of effort seems to make progress, it may be worth changing your strategy. However, if you find yourself hopping from strategy to strategy, that's telling you something. It's telling you that, maybe, you're in the wrong arena.

CHOOSE YOUR ARENA

There will be moments in life when we realize we are playing the wrong sport. There will come a time when we need to change our strategy, instead of practicing more and more.

You're not getting as much engagement on Instagram. The lackluster response isn't exciting you anymore. So you decide to switch over to TikTok to gamble for the quick fix of the easy win.

The question you need to ask yourself anytime you trade one strategy for another is, "Am I doing this for the right reasons? Is this issue with my current strategy that it's not the right fit, or am I just getting sloppy in my execution?"

Who are you? The person who, on a swing and a miss, gets a bucket of balls and gets to work on the range? Someone who says:

"I'm going to work on this."
"I'm going to film myself."
"I'm going to see what's going on."
"I am going to correct that behavior until it is going right all of the time on the practice range, and then I'm going to get back out and play my game."

When you're met with resistance, decide who you are. Choose your arena and do the work to be that person.

We all have these gut check moments frequently in marketing and in leadership. We have times where what we're doing feels like it isn't working anymore. We have times where we feel like we're not good enough, when we're so early in the process and ask, "Did I choose the wrong path, or am I simply afraid of the obstacle in front of me?"

Restarting is very exciting. The desire to restart, to set things back to that initial energy, is a real temptation for law firm owners. It can be a real high to get that flush of entrepreneurial spirit when it was just you and a laptop in a rented room, hustling it out.

This is the most difficult part. Maybe your instincts are right. Maybe you should switch sports, but have you done the analysis to know that it's the right choice?

Have you looked at it and found the core flaw behind why it didn't work? Was it the system or was it your technique? Have you proven it really is the wrong sport for your skillset?

If we have picked the wrong sport, we then have to ask which one is right for you? What plays to your skill sets. What marketing channel, systems channel, email strategy, et cetera, should you produce with your skill set? You need to pick one, conducive to you, to play to your strengths.

So, for example, if you're really good at building professional relationships, LinkedIn or Facebook may be a good platform for you. If you're entertaining and engaging, producing videos on YouTube might be where you thrive. Regardless, you need to pick a space where you continue to produce. You really love writing? Focus on email and direct mail. Find where you're comfortable. Find where you are confident. Find where you are capable and put that to work for you.

MAKE IT A PRACTICE

You will encounter people who, just like in the sports world, are amazing at multiple sports. We look at them with a touch of envy. Things seem to just come easy to them. Say what you want about the Kansas City Chiefs, and I'll say a lot as a Denver Broncos fan, but their quarterback, Patrick Mahomes, deserves a level of respect. Not only is he an exceptional NFL quarterback, but he could also have become an equally great baseball player. That's true of a lot of quarterbacks in the NFL.

We look at those people, who excel in multiple fields, and we want to do the same. The reality is, if you try to be great at everything you'll end up mediocre at most.

Once you find your arena, you need to put in your reps and perfect your form. You need to make it a practice.

Once you reframe it as something to perfect over time, failure stops being scary. Instead, it develops an excitement all its own. It allows you to start competing against yourself and experimenting with how to improve. When your new post only gets a few likes, after a streak of several hundred likes and shares, rather than get defeated you ask yourself, "Why?" You question, and you get better.

It stops being a matter of you, individually, not being good enough and instead allows you to set a standard for the work you are putting out. Suddenly, it's the result that's not good enough and you're inspired to push to figure out how to find a better outcome. Once you find that drive for yourself, it's time to pass it on to others.

PASS IT ON TO YOUR TEAM

If you're the type of leader who is demanding, hard-driving, and believe that's the best way to be, then don't play soft with your team. I'm not telling you to yell at them but make it a performance culture. Cultivate a team that is willing to put in hard work and reap the rewards from it. Set expectations and form a roster that is willing to live up to them.

Put your best skills forward in marketing and leadership. Put yourself in the right sport. Most of all, when you get knocked down, decide who you are. Decide whether or not you are supposed to get up again, and when you do never let them keep you down.

And if you're struggling? If you can't seem to find where your skills might get you or that gut-check moment is stopping you in your tracks, that's okay. We can help you with that. That is what we do through Law firm Alchemy. We help people become that fully realized version of themselves. We help them become the sort of people who, when they meet a gut-check moment they say,

"That's fine. I got this. I'm good. What else you got?"

If you're excited, if you're interested, if you're eager to improve, sign up on our email list. Hear more ideas and insights, and if you're interested in potentially pursuing some form of coaching, consulting, or courses, please reach out. You don't have to be in the arena alone, and I'd love to see you win.

ALCHEMY IN ACTION:

Lean into the resistance: When progress gets hard, keep going.

Choose your arena: Find the area you want to thrive and stick with it.

CLAIM $729 IN FREE RESOURCES
TO GET MORE CLIENTS, RECLAIM YOUR TIME, AND BUILD YOUR IDEAL LAW FIRM...

Add fuel to your entrepreneurial fire with our collection of guides, templates, and how-to information, guaranteed to help you:

- Generate high-quality, pre-sold leads for your law firm (so you can stop worrying about whether or not the phone is going to ring this week)

- Improve your leadership skills through superior communication techniques (which translate just as well to communication with a spouse or partner)

- Take back control of your marketing (including how to communicate with and hold your vendors accountable)

- Develop a stronger brand message (with a big, bold promise)

- Master your core financial numbers (so your firm runs like a well-oiled, profit-generating machine instead of a "what's happened lately" patchwork of decisions)

- And more!

This package of resources is exclusively for readers of this book, and to claim yours, just go to:

WWW.LAWFIRMALCHEMY.COM/VOLUME1

Go right now to get your hands on these free gifts for you!

chapter 21

MAXIMIZING TIME AND HABITS
WITH EMILY STEDMAN

Emily Stedman represents a wide range of clients, both small businesses and international corporations, at all phases of sophisticated commercial litigation, from investigation to appeal, in state and federal courts. Appreciated for her creative problem-solving skills, Emily regularly identifies practical and customized solutions for clients on a wide range of matters.

Emily understands that litigation can sidetrack a company's goals and focus. She aims to collaborate as both a legal advisor and business partner to keep client business on balance during the interruption of litigation. In addition to her legal skills, Emily studied the science behind well-being at Yale and is invested in learning about time management, efficiency, and organization, as well as how these day-to-day struggles can be optimized. Emily enjoys working closely with clients to find the best path forward.

I'VE BEEN IN A BIG FIRM for eight years. I've struggled with the emotional weight and isolation which often comes from being a lawyer trying to prove his or her value in a workplace with a lot of other high-performers. A lot of people build good habits but they never build a good system to support those habits. They're miserable because of it.

The legal workspace is hard. It's so easy for the professional to co-mingle with the personal, and both end up suffering for it. A lot of people have a difficult time living and working in this environment. It causes stress. It causes fatigue. It can cause the development of some unhealthy coping mechanisms.

Let me give you a lifeline and tell you, your work does not need to make you miserable. I've spent years experimenting and discovering methods to cope with the stress and demands this work can put on you. I've taken to sharing what I've learned across various platforms, and I'm elated to share some of it with you in this chapter. Your experiences are valid, and you don't need to carry all this weight on your shoulders. This chapter is going to focus on several things I've seen other lawyers, me included, struggle with. If you're like so many who have struggled, hopefully it can serve as the first steps or reaffirmation of building a happier, and more productive workspace. For me, it all begins with time.

I'm in a big firm, so I have a billable hour requirement. Even if there's no requirement, a lot of attorneys are living in the *bill by the hour, or 0.1 increments* mentality. I find it helpful, not only so I can have something clear to put on an invoice for my clients, but also as a helpful habit to track my time. For me, it's not just about meeting a requirement, *it's about showing my value.*

SHOWING YOUR VALUE WITH BILLING

Billable time can be a bit of a taboo term. It has certain connotations, good and bad. I don't like to approach it from a place of judgement. A billable hour is not a good thing, or a bad thing. It's just data. It's information.

I'm sure we could devote an entire chapter as to whether or not firms should have a billable hour requirement but as of now it's a reality of the industry, so a best practice is learning how to make it work for you and not the other way around.

I struggled for three years before I heard someone talk about strategies to simplify how to monitor your hours. They recommended breaking your hours down from the standard yearly goal into monthly, weekly and even daily goals. It changed my life, and since then it's been the standard way I've recorded my hours. I've never missed a goal. Even in the most difficult seasons of my career, the hardship has never had to do with my billable hours. It's become a constant. It's become synonymous with stability. It was a system I immediately implemented and never looked back. To be a highly effective associate, start with the billable hour. Start with time.

For starters, **track everything**.

I track everything I do, all day, in 0.1 Increments. Whether it's billable or not. If it is billable, bill it. This allows the partner to see everything you're doing. It shows you're accounting for your time and gives them concrete data to facilitate future conversations. *Are you billing enough? Are you billing too little? What do your narratives look like?*

A lot of associates discount their time. They become unsure of themselves. They think they're taking too long, or billing too much. Sometimes it might be the case, but nine times out of ten they underestimate and undervalue the work they're doing. I encourage associates not to discount their time. Unless a partner comes to them and says otherwise, bill for your billable time. Otherwise you're only doing a disservice to yourself. You're not even giving the client or the partner an opportunity to get time paid for. You're discounting yourself before you ever get out of the gate.

You have to adjust your mindset. If you're not billing them, it demonstrates you're not doing work for the client. The client has hired you to handle a legal situation. **Your billable hours are the proof of the value and length to which you're working for the client.**

It's okay, and essential, to charge money for the time you spend working on a case. In many ways, if you're an associate, it's your role to bill time in order to demonstrate what you're doing and generate business. I work in a huge firm. There are a lot of other people doing the same work I am. As I've developed this plan, what's really helped me is to view myself as a solo practitioner. When I'm working, I'm the entrepreneur and this is my business. When I bill my time, I'm not just showing the client, but also the partner what I'm doing and demonstrating my value. Your billable hours shouldn't solely be about doing the work, it should be about showing your work.

Developing a systematic, habitual approach to recording my time is well-suited to my personality. I'm extremely Type-A. Hell, I'm borderline neurotic. I understand developing a systematic daily habit like time recording is the opposite of what some people see as valuable or helpful.

By creating a system where I enter my time daily, my timesheet stops being a chore and becomes something more. It becomes a perpetual to-do list for the week. It becomes a compass which keeps me on course. As I track my time through every step of the billable year it alleviates an incredible amount of stress and uncertainty. I never have to worry about what to do next, or what's coming up. The steps are there. I don't have to focus on billable time because it's become an afterthought.

Suddenly, I'm able to focus on the work. Because I have a system in place, I can free up time. I can devote time to things which recharge me when I'm ahead when things are slow. It's always hard work, but it's the right sort of hard. It can be difficult to implement, but what it can do for you long term is exponential and will add massive, progressive benefits to how you work. We all want to be our best selves at work.

Whatever habits you adopt, devote yourself to the trial and error of finding what's best for you. Leave the rest behind. At every stage in life, you'll see people performing their best. Oftentimes, it might seem like they have everything figured out. You might feel miles behind them. The truth is, everyone is fighting different battles. Don't spend your time trying to carbon copy someone else's version of work onto yours. You'll be miserable every time. You'll get stuck in a loop of cognitive dissonance. Devote yourself to your own personal journey, while still honoring theirs. Experiment and implement what works for you, until the biggest struggles are an automatic success.

HANDLING HARD EMOTIONS IN THE WORKPLACE

Despite appearances, no one really has it fully together. Everyone's got their own personal battle. You never know what's going on behind the scenes of someone's life. There is a semi-toxic mindset when it comes to "leaving work at work, and your personal life at home." The reality is, it's not possible. The two interweave and bleed into one another and, sometimes, things bubble over the surface.

I tend to be someone who exudes a sense of having it all together. I assure you, it couldn't be further from the truth. I'm anxious. I'm critical of myself. I struggle with a lot of the same issues young lawyers face. When I first joined a big firm there would be several times a week where you'd find me behind a closed door, fighting back tears, feeling like I was the only one making mistakes. After talking to others, I realized a lot of us were feeling the same way. Peak behind 95% of the closed doors of an American law firm, and you'll find a young associate struggling with self-doubt and what being successful means to them, and to their small firm.

Rather than push everything I was feeling under the surface, I took the shared experience myself and so many other attorneys were having and I started talking about it publicly. I posted about it on LinkedIn. Surprisingly, people really started to respond and engage with the content. Doors opened. It started to feel safe to go to those heavy places.

I now work in an incredible firm. They're extremely supportive. It's filled with people like me. Any work culture can be slow to change. Any industry can be set in their ways. A lot of places aren't necessarily ready to invite an open environment where people can talk about emotions and their work, but those places do exist.

The pandemic changed the way we approach work. There's a perspective shift happening. Whether it's the changes from the pandemic or newer generations coming into the workplace, mental health is becoming something more and more championed. If firms can create an environment where we feel safe being vulnerable, and speaking up, it could really change the overall culture of your business and increase retention at the same time.

Emotions are a natural, human response. People cry. People get angry. People laugh. If you work anywhere long enough, you're going to weather some heavy emotions between you and your colleagues. If someone's displaying emotion in front of you it means they either are comfortable enough to be vulnerable, or they're experiencing so much stress the emotions boil over. When it happens to me, I try to follow the lead of the person experiencing an emotional response. I try not to shut down. I try to sit with them. I validate their emotional reaction while simultaneously trying not to put any weight behind what's causing it. I don't think it should be a surprise if certain people don't feel the same comfort around emotions. Displaying emotions might make some people uncomfortable. Some emotional responses, like yelling or screaming, will never be acceptable in the workplace. Still, it happens, but leaning into healthier emotional responses can prevent the bigger blowups which disrupt productivity and safety in the workplace.

Emotions are universal to being human, no matter the workplace. At the end of the day, underneath every attorney is another human being. We all have lives. We all have dreams. We all want happiness. The profession is changing, and law firms who change with it will have a leg up in the end. The legal industry has been a heavily male dominated field. With every year, there are more and more firms owned and operated by women. Which is awesome. Anger tends to get associated with masculine energy, whereas compassion and the act of nurturing is more feminine. There's a disruption to what's often been categorized as "the old boys club" and a re-education needs to happen. We need distance from typically masculine anger and step closer to feminine compassion. We're in an industry of people. We have to get comfortable with people being people.

In terms of masculine and feminine energy, we need to have a little of both. Science shows it. When I talk about the two, I'm not necessarily speaking about gender. Another way of phrasing it could be *hard* energy and *soft*. For a long time, if a woman didn't fit into certain spaces she needed to lean into the hard energy of the environment. I think, now, there's room to meet in the middle. There's a benefit to meeting in the middle.

Men can embrace the softer energy of the space. It's not a matter of one being right and the other being wrong. It's about finding an environment where everyone feels safe. It's about finding an environment where everyone benefits, where everyone succeeds.

Anxiety is common in the workplace. It manifests regardless of the masculine or feminine energy of a space. Everyone benefits from understanding that anxiety is universal. Rather than going down the path of ignoring it, it's possible to learn from it

When I was in the first grade, my teacher pulled me aside and told me, "You're going to go gray really early if you don't stop worrying." I've always been anxious. Regardless, I navigated high school, college, teaching, law school and finally my profession and I got by. You eventually develop a kind of superpower, being constantly productive despite a voice in your ear constantly telling you, "You're not good enough."

There have been so many seasons of my life when I was convinced I was failing at everything. I was my harshest critic. I began to disassociate. I've spent nearly all my years in big law with a therapist. As a result, I began to be more open about my anxieties and feelings of inadequacy. What most surprised me is that when you open a dialogue about your shortcomings, people are open about sharing theirs. Healing starts to happen.

Anxiety doesn't make you weak, or any less of a high performer. It's important to hold onto both. You can be anxious. The work can be hard. You can still love it and be fulfilled. Things can be hard, and you can survive. Things can be hard, and you can thrive.

CLARIFYING EXPECTATIONS

It shocked me when I joined a firm. I had no idea how to do this. A partner would say,

"We have to get something to the client by Friday. Can you have it to me by Tuesday?" You say,

"Great." You get it to them by Tuesday and hear crickets. Wednesday comes around and you still haven't heard anything. Friday morning arrives and you haven't seen any movement.

Whose responsibility is it, at this point? Is it yours, or the partner's responsibility to follow up?

A lot of high achieving, type A people, feel anxious to come across as a nag or bother. In this situation, a lot of lawyers will say, "I did my part. I got it to them when they asked. It's in their court now." They honored their commitment but they also contributed to something which can be problematic in the workplace. *It's not my problem, now. It's not my job.*

Inevitably when that happens, it's the client who suffers. It falls to taking ownership of the work you do. Communication, and setting expectations, are key to successfully collaborating in a workplace. Sometimes it means nagging and bothering to ensure you're doing your job. Pester away. Get comfortable with it. You're helping the entire team keep deadlines.

It's a practice. I've gotten to the point where I am comfortable enough with crucial communication that I'll utilize what I call **negative notice.**

> *If I don't hear from you by XYZ time,*
> *I am going to do ABC action.*

It's usually enough to get someone's attention, and you don't need to spend any wasted time feeling anxious you aren't being heard, or the work is not getting done.

All of these strategies are meant to empower, and enable, people to thrive in their chosen work environments. The world is changing and, contrary to what a lot of people say, it does not need to change for the worse. Develop the habits and practices to make yourself an incredible legal producer, with a vibrant life both professionally and personally.

ALCHEMY IN ACTION:

Billable time: Track your billable time as a means to keep yourself on task, and show your value.

Manage emotions: Recognize emotions are a natural human response, hold space for people and honor their experiences in whatever way you are comfortable.

Clarify expectations: Develop techniques to ensure there is follow through on work you are completing.

chapter 22

EXPANDING YOUR REACH
WITH KELLAM T. PARKS

Kellam Parks *began his legal career with a mid-sized firm doing primarily insurance defense work and moved through a number of local firms seeking the right fit of practice areas, camaraderie, and compensation. He eventually decided to go out on his own, founding the Law Office of Kellam T. Parks, PLLC in January 2012.*

One of the motivating factors of forming his own firm was to integrate modern technologies into his practice, which was hard to do in a larger firm. Kellam created the law firm to be paperless with cloud-based systems to enable immediate and remote access for himself and his clients. This has served the firm well as it transitioned over time to Parks Zeigler, PLLC, a firm in 2024 of 13 lawyers, 36 people, and three offices across two states. The attorneys and staff are able to utilize digital technologies for all aspects of the practice of law, from legal research to trial presentation. The law firm is also able to harness the power of social media to inform the public on the attorneys'

> *practice areas and keep in touch with their clients. Kellam's focus on technology keeps him up to date on the latest issues involving cybersecurity and data privacy, allowing him to best serve clients in this area of his practice.*

I HAVE ENTREPRENEURSHIP in my blood. My father owned several businesses in his lifetime. He learned early on he preferred to work for himself. He sold used cars. He sold clothes. He owned a car repair shop and, when he retired, he sold that. My dad sold. My mom had a crafting business. She built stuff, developed a reputation around the various craft shows. Both had their own versions of successes. They were never taught it. They received lessons you can't pick up in school, but they still wanted something more for their kids.

I'm the first in my immediate family to go to college, and then to law school. It's what my parents wanted; they said, "You need to go to college. You need to get a good job in XYZ." They never encouraged me down the path to entrepreneurship, nor did I ever imagine it would be a road I'd follow. Looking back though, it was inevitable.

I branched out on my own with a solo firm over a decade ago. It took years to figure out exactly how I wanted to do it. I worked at a number of law firms. There was a lot I liked about them, but I wanted to do things my way, a different way. I learned this lesson a little later than my dad did. I wanted to work for myself, but I had to figure out how.

When I went to law school in the late 1990s, they taught you almost nothing about running a business. We had a legal skills course where you learned what a trust account was and talked you through imagined scenarios where you own your own firm, but that was the extent of it. In those days maybe everybody assumed you were going to work for the government or work for another firm. There just wasn't a focus on entrepreneurship. There was zero discussion about how to get clients, how to run a law firm, and especially how to market.

I couldn't do any of it, and I wasn't learning it once I entered the professional world. It was one of the growing lists of reasons I wanted to do things my way. These days, I know a lot more than I did when I started. If I had known half of what I know now when I began, the journey would have gotten me farther, faster, and with a lot less stress along the way. I now prefer the business of law to the mechanics of practicing law. I spend more of my time running my firm, working on the systems, procedures, tech, and most importantly the people.

This chapter is about how I got to this point, and the lessons, stories, and insight I picked up along the way.

DECIDE WHAT YOU ENJOY, HIRE THE REST

What I always tell lawyers who ask me about law firm ownership, whether they are starting out or years ahead of me, is **decide what you enjoy**. My co-owner, for instance, loves practicing law. He loves trying cases. He loves dusting it up. He loves going to court. He's a fantastic litigator. I really don't anymore. I litigated my whole career – 24+ years. I just don't enjoy it like I used to.

When I practice, I prefer collaboration and the areas of law which invite collaboration. While I still handle a few high-asset divorces and other complex civil litigation, I now primarily focus my practice on cybersecurity and data privacy. It's mostly business consulting and development. There are so many avenues you can go down practicing law, and so many people pigeonhole themselves into a box; whether it's what they started doing, what they think they should or must do, or what is currently making them money. A lot of them are miserable. Decide what you want to do. Do what you like and ignite your passion. If you want to practice law, and you enjoy practicing law, follow your passion, and hire people to do the rest. Hire talented, experienced businesspeople to run your firm.

You can be a great practicing attorney. You can be a great firm owner. It is extremely difficult to be both at the same time. I certainly learned that lesson. I started as a solo, and right from the start I knew I needed help. I reached out to my older sister, Deb, and convinced her to move back to the area to be my right hand. Within the first three years I hired an assistant, a paralegal, an associate attorney, and a full-time marketing manager. Hiring people, especially when you're just starting out, can be scary. You'll find a million reasons why hiring additional staff isn't a good idea, but there's only one reason you need to bring people on: **the right people will help you grow.**

BUILDING AN EFFECTIVE PARTNERSHIP

My firm eventually went from me as the sole owner to a partnership, and an incredibly effective one at that. My co-owner, Brandon, and I practiced law at two previous firms together. He is a good friend, and almost as soon as we joined forces, we started gaining momentum and growing. We brought on additional staff. We split the work into what excited both of us. We took off. We're both business oriented. Brandon was a partner at the firm I had left to start my firm. A few years after my departure, he asked if we could get together for a drink. He wanted to explore starting his own firm and while he was business savvy, he had never run his own firm – I knew the tech and some experience to share. However, during the conversation, we started discussing perhaps a partnership instead. Brandon laid it out beautifully. He summarized everything with three questions I needed to ask myself:

"Do you want a partner?"

"If so, would you want to partner with me – are our philosophies/visions aligned?"

"If yes to both, can we work out the details?"

Interestingly, the last bit was the easiest to work out once I decided I could have a partner. The longest discussions were the middle part – the philosophies and visions. It's essential, with any partnership, to make sure you share the same goals. Goals will change over time, it's not about them always staying the same from the word "go." It's more about the alignment of your goals and attuning them as you grow the business together. Nearly a decade later and we still make this a priority to stay on track of what we both want from the business. We have a weekly leadership meeting with our COO and then have quarterly all-day meetings with our business coach to dive in deep on these important topics.

There are so many advantages to a good partnership. The first, from a purely mercenary standpoint, is that black and white difference it can make in your numbers. You have someone else entirely committed to the business because they own it too. My partner is a rainmaker, a huge generator of work. He shares my strong work ethic and has a great reputation within our community. Another benefit is you have someone who is working toward the same goals as you but approaches it in a different way. My partner and I are both good trial attorneys, but he approaches things with a 'big picture' approach, while I tend to be more detail oriented. We get to the same place but on different paths. I jokingly call him 'controlled chaos', whereas I plan everything. He's the Ying to my Yang. I believe the best partner is someone who thinks and works differently than you do. It will fill your toolbox with an entirely fresh set of viewpoints, perspectives, and skillsets.

As someone who likes to have <u>all</u> of the information, my partner pushes me, and I likewise pull him back as he likes to move forward quickly. We balance each other out and things work well. What I gained right away from merging forces with Brandon was a force of forward momentum. I'm a Type A perfectionist, which frankly can be a business killer. You can't operate a business if you wait for every bit of information and suffer from paralysis from analysis. Perfect is the enemy of good. Thankfully, I've learned how to overcome my natural inclinations and get <u>enough</u> information and then just act.

Brandon and I make up for one another's shortcomings and amplify each other's strengths. We run in different circles. We have different contacts. We have different skill sets when it comes to the practice of law. The last benefit to having an effective partner is having someone to talk to. It's incredibly valuable to be able to approach a problem from more than one angle, and to talk to someone who thinks differently from the way you do. Thanks to our partnership, we've really been able to push forward to get to where we are today.

KNOWING WHEN TO INSTALL C LEVEL EXECUTIVES

I would love to tell you that tremendous strategy and brilliant forethought went into securing a chief operating officer and executive business coach. The truth is, despite having a successful law firm, the apple cart's wheels were coming off. The tent was on fire. While Brandon and I managed to do a pretty good job getting us to where we were, we couldn't keep it up – running the firm, practicing law, and sleeping every now and again was too much. We needed help. Don't be like us. Don't let your tent catch fire before you call for help.

We opened a couple offices, which gave us a new level of challenges, and we implemented some technologies and management systems which, in hindsight, created more problems than they solved. Knowing we needed help, we first did a national search to bring on a COO. We interviewed numerous candidates and ended up finding someone literally right down the street from us. She had an executive MBA from the College of William and Mary, was a CPA by training, and had experience as a COO for a few medical practices, and finally, a medical device company which she helped take public. She had a ton of hands-on experience with operations and just needed to learn the legal industry and our practice.

We got to the size where chief executive leadership made sense. A COO is expensive. It's certainly not the first full-time position you need to fill. Even if you're pushing beyond seven figures as a firm, there are different options to make it more economically viable. More and more firms and individuals offer fractional executive services on a contractual basis, giving you access to the benefits while keeping a conservative hand on the possible expense. Make the best choice for your business.

In my experience, most lawyers are not fantastic business-people. It's not their fault, we're not taught this stuff in law school. Though, in hindsight having done it now for over a decade, I'm not sure a lot of it can be taught. There's no formalized path to success. Every journey is different. Every lawyer is different. Gaining the education to thrive in the world of law firm ownership comes, in many respects, after law school.

EXPANDING YOUR FIRM, EXPANDING YOUR REACH

I like to say we grow our firm with a three-legged stool approach. The first leg is expanding our existing areas of practice and adding new ones that make sense for us, the second is expanding into new geographic regions, and the third is finding older lawyers that want to slow down or retire and fold them into the practice. A lot of people advise specializing in one or two specific areas of the law, so our expansion moved slightly counter to conventional wisdom. As a rule, specializing works.

It's easier to niche. It's easier to market. You can stand out and gain notoriety for one specific thing. But it's just not what we wanted to do.

My partner and I have practiced in numerous different areas of the law our entire careers. It's what we fell into. It's what we're passionate about. When we got together, we didn't have the detailed business plan we have now. We knew we wanted to grow, but the exact plan wasn't necessarily there. We just wanted to do good work, make good money, and figure the rest out as we went. It worked for us. People saw the work we were doing, and in an organic way, began pursuing work with us.

The first part of our growth began by finding experienced lawyers with a good reputation and book of business who practiced in an area of law we did or were willing to expand into, who were unhappy where they were and then making an offer for them to join us. We found that often it wasn't about the money – they wanted more freedom, better technology, or a better work environment (and, sometimes, too, it was about the money).

The second part of our growth came from knowing a local attorney that had her own firm who was interested in becoming a judge. Running your firm and having to shut it down should that goal be met is daunting. Easier to not have the stresses and hassle of administration. She folded her practice into ours and that gave us our second location in a neighboring city. Later we had the opportunity to expand into a second state because an attorney we knew wanted to open an office there and his former firm didn't have the same vision as he did. We provided the opportunity and support. It all comes down to finding the right people in the practice areas and expanding, supporting them, and then looking to an area for the resources to expand. Our goal is to find somebody who is a well-known entity in the area. We look for someone who knows the players, knows the courts, and has a name.

The third leg of our stool is to find older attorneys who want to slow down. Most attorneys do not build a practice that can be sold – they are the practice. Rather than closing their practice, which for a solo attorney means losing your income, we want to invite these attorneys to join our law firm. Their job changes into becoming a rainmaker and mentor. They can practice as much or as little as they want. We end up providing a continued source of income and providing benefits, and we gain institutional knowledge and generation of clients, which helps us grow. We're still working on this third leg of the stool but are confident we'll find the right fit in the near future.

The practice of law is demanding and owning your own law firm is that much harder. I've found the key to success and making it work is finding what works for you. Figure out what you want – do you want to practice law, run the firm, or both? Do you want to be a solo, a small firm, or create a sprawling legal empire? Once you figure out what you want, you can then work toward achieving that vision. If you don't know where you're going, how are you going to get there?

ALCHEMY IN ACTION:

Decide what you enjoy: Invest your energy in what you enjoy doing, and hire out the rest.

Build an effective partnership: The right people will help you grow.

Determine your leadership needs: Determine when, and how best, to onboard executive leadership.

Expand your reach: Expand geographically, and with new areas of practice that interest you.

chapter 23

BUILDING BETTER HABITS
WITH JESSICA HARRINGTON

> *Jessica Harrington (MPH)* is an in-demand speaker on the topics of stress management and burnout for customer service and blue collar companies. Her six-month workshop, *Journey to Yourself,* focuses on developing healthy, constrictive habits and tools for employees.

I GREW UP IN an addiction household, so I started my career in the addiction field. I was working with men, reducing their sentence from jail. Working out of rehab facilities, what stood out to me most was my clients and my coworkers shared the exact same stressors. Despite the different perspectives, different roles, different places, they were suffering the same strain. The difference was that my coworkers could go to the bar after work to decompress. My clients weren't allowed to. It was a different judgment for them. They weren't able to handle their stress. They had a 'problem'. They couldn't manage their life.

That's when I decided to go back to school for Public Health. I wanted to focus on prevention. Addiction is the result of not being taught the tools to handle stress. In the absence of the right tools people turn to what's in their environment, what's easy and available. Some people might dive into work, some people might dive into helping others. Some people might dive into drinking, or substances. Society judges which tools are acceptable and which aren't.

Humans are creatures of habit, specifically the habits that have been the most prominently reinforced. The problems in our lives culminate from the buildup of destructive habits while success is the result of constructive habits. The key to success for so many plans for recovery, whether it's a twelve-step program or a pathway to get out of debt, is that they are built with small, incremental changes in mind. One day at a time. Do the next right thing. The genius behind this perspective, and why it's worked for so many people, is it takes willpower out of the equation. You don't need to have the willpower to create lasting, and perpetual, change. You just need the willpower to tackle this next moment.

Since this mindset is so effective in the treatment of destructive habits then, inversely, it is equally effective in the forming of constructive habits. It's effective in forming who we most desire to become.

INTERSECTIONS OF STRESS

You're a very busy law firm owner. You're managing the entire firm and, on top of that, you're still a practicing attorney handling cases yourself. You struggle with your identity as a business owner, a lawyer, a spouse, and a parent. You're burning yourself out, maybe you're turning to some not-so-healthy habits. You're constantly choosing fast food over healthier options. Every evening you're unwinding with mindless television and several fingers of whiskey. Things that were once occasional indulgences become daily essentials as you try to cope with the stress. You're unhappy. Your family is unhappy. Your spouse is unhappy. You find yourself looking into the mirror and asking,

"How did I let myself get to this point?"

The example is a little extreme but all of those examples are common problems my clients arrive with, and they're common among individuals in high-performing professions. The struggle to address problems with stress, identity, family, and health when there is already so much on your plate can be overwhelming.

Thankfully there are solutions. Thankfully there's help.

The first thing I ask new clients is: Where do you feel the stress in your life? Anyone can look at that previous example and say, "Oh there's an obvious issue with balance. With identity, etc." but, the issues we struggle with can often get distorted when we're the ones experiencing them.

Spend time reflecting on it. Make a list and zero in on where you're feeling stress in your life. If you come up with a few different sources, find the place where they intersect. We can feel stress, strain and fatigue coming from a lot of different places. When we do, it makes the weight of all the stress so much more overwhelming. If we look a little closer those different places where we feel stress intersect into one or two things that are either missing in our lives or are detrimentally present.

Step one is clearly identifying where you're feeling the stress and where those stressors intersect. Once you do, you can start the work to find the remedy.

START SMALL

You've decided your greatest stressor is your health. You're not fitting into clothes that used to feel tailor-made for you. Your spouse is starting to make little comments about the extra weight you're wearing. You're getting winded when you play with your kids. All of this adds up and can add chronic stress to your life.

The first question, after you've found your stressors, is: How are you taking care of yourself?

Adults spend so much of their time showing up for everyone else. We get into the habit of neglecting, even abandoning, ourselves so that the needs of everyone around us can be met. If you're suffering from chronic stress, it's time to focus on how you can show up for yourself. It's like the oxygen mask on the airplane; you put yours on first before you look at anyone else.

Along the same line, the change you make in your life to alleviate stress and build better habits has to be for you and you alone.

If you want to get healthy so someone else thinks you look good, you'll miss out on the opinion of the person who matters most: You.

If you're making healthy dietary choices so someone will get off your case, you'll just get better at sneaking those indulgences when no one is looking.

Change has to start with you and is the most lasting when it's being done for yourself.

When you're ready to make that change, start small. Start with one small action you can take to bring you closer to your goal.

Get up from your desk twice a day,
and walk for ten minutes.

Maybe that seems too small but, trust me, starting small means there's room to grow. Here's what's important. When you're walking, check in with yourself.

How does your body feel? Where are you feeling tension
in your body? If you can really feel it in a specific place,
what does stretching do to alleviate it?

Take a moment to leave work behind, and just become familiar with your body again. There is a huge connection between the kinesthetic, the mental and the emotional. When we work sedentary jobs, our prime focus becomes the mental and emotional. We shut the door on examining where we're carrying tension in our bodies. Taking the time to move helps us unlock secret stress we didn't realize we were carrying in our bodies. The biggest question to ask yourself during your daily devotional to moving is:

Am I enjoying this?

Walking may not be your thing, and that's fine! At the end of the day it's not about the activity, it's about moving. Maybe after a week, you realize what you need is to stretch, or jog, or shadowbox, or tai chi.

It truly does not matter. What matters is that you open that dialogue with yourself. You take that first small step and, after taking it, you remain open to taking another.

KEEP THE GOAL IN FRONT OF YOU

A month in, you're feeling pretty good. You're moving more. You're more in tune with yourself, but you're still seeing places where old habits are winning. Your diet still needs work. Maybe you're constantly turning to the coffeepot or sugary energy drinks to get through the day, leaving you vacillating between vibrating anxiety and midday crashes. Now that you're moving more, it's time to turn to your diet. Rather than create a broad goal like, "Drink more water." Try this instead:

*I'm going to keep a full glass of water
on my desk, at all times.*

Here's what's wonderful about that. If it's in front of you, it's going to become your go to solution far more often. Since the goal is to keep it full, once you've drained the glass, you'll stay driven to fill it up again. It gets to be reinforcing. It gets to be a fun game. It gets to be a habit.

Do that for a bit and, a week or so later, put an apple or carrots next to it. The same principles apply. When the healthy choice stays in front of you, it's easier to choose it. Outside of your snacks, find a different place to eat your meals. Don't eat at your desk.

YOU ARE HOW YOU EAT

We all know the phrase,

"You are what you eat." But how we eat equally informs how we show up for ourselves. When you make your meal an accessory to whatever else you're doing, especially working, you stop thinking about it. You're still working. You're not actually enjoying that meal that you worked to afford, to make, that you made time to make yourself. You aren't present with yourself.

How many times did you eat like you were in jail?

Something happens to your brain when you step away. It gives you a chance to reset. It gives you the opportunity to come up for air and look at the big picture. You think to check in with your spouse. You realize you were sitting with your legs crossed the entire time and your muscles are tight.

Suddenly, because you took that extra five minutes to pause, you gave your attention to preventing future strain on yourself.

MAKE IT ABOUT YOU

I'm not telling you to make the selfish choice. I'm saying when you start to learn about yourself, and about what you really need, advocate for yourself. If I'm doing everything for everybody else, or for my business, or for my family, I'm not doing anything for me. When I start to learn what I need and want, I need to be able to create time and space for those needs.

It becomes essential not only to communicate those desires, but to establish boundaries and hold them. Maintaining those essential boundaries will not only keep resentment or frustration from building up, it will also keep you on a forward trajectory to continue your personal growth.

Boundaries are less about holding people or experiences at arm's length and more about establishing guard rails along your personalized road towards growth.

There will always be something. As an entrepreneur, there is always something to do. It might be a conference, a work lunch, a social event, whatever it is, if it doesn't align with the direction you're headed, keep your eye on your own individual goal.

There doesn't need to be malice in it. There doesn't need to be an apology in it. It can be as simple as,

"That's not something I can do right now. Are there some other ways I can support you?" The latter part of that is entirely optional. That's the beauty of a boundary. It's not about why you can or can't do something. The only thing that matters is what you can or can't do.

MAKE LASTING CHANGE

We all love building habits. How do you get them to stick? How can we make habits last longer? I tell people, if you want to run a marathon you're not going to just sign up and go tomorrow.

You have to buy the shoes. You have to stretch. Then, you have to walk. When you build a business, you don't just balloon to six figures overnight. Those kinds of stories aren't real. It's a process. It's about systems. It's realizing that the habits you build are an entire toolbox, rather than just one tool. After all, if your only tool is a hammer, everything in life becomes a nail.

Build your toolbox. Fill it over. Learn how you love to move. Learn what leaves you feeling centered. Find what recharges you and know what drains you. With the right tools in place, you'll be able to fix anything and lay the foundation of real, positive change.

ALCHEMY IN ACTION:

Intersecting stress: Identify where the different stressors in your life meet.

Start small: Introduce small, easily obtainable habits and gradually scale up.

Keep the goal in front of you: Let your positive habits have a front row seat.

Make it about you: Take care of yourself first, so you can take care of others.

Make lasting change: Fill your emotional toolbox with a variety of tools.

chapter 24

TAKING ACTION
– CHARLEY

As we round third towards the home plate of Volume One of this book, I'd like to talk a little bit about a subject which is particularly important to me: **Taking action**.

In this profession, maybe in every profession, there is a lot of self-bullying that happens. There is a lot of self-shaming surrounding action. I once had a conversation with a client who focuses primarily on estate planning. He came to one of our calls and brought up an action item that we had placed on a previous call. He hadn't done it, or at least, he hadn't done the 100% version of the action. Instead, he'd accomplished maybe a 20% version.

What's interesting is that in the past, clients like him would come to me and maybe just wouldn't have taken any action outright because they were afraid of only doing the small version. Their hope was, by doing literally nothing, they could sweep it under the rug or litigate away the necessity of the action.

Nothing was better than something if they couldn't accomplish all.

That perspective really boggles me. This is a common phenomenon. Obviously, coaching lawyers with litigation experience, they'll be able to explain away why they didn't take action. Everywhere else we have a simpler definition: making excuses.

Which one ultimately is better for your future litigating: Making excuses or taking the 20%? If you run the ball 20 yards instead of into the end zone, you're still 20 yards closer to the goal post.

By walking up to the brink of taking action, by giving this moment of discovery for ourselves, we can find when the path we chose was not the correct path for ourselves. There is a pattern which can happen when we get so busy explaining away why something has not been done. We end up giving away the power of execution, the power of taking baby steps. We lose the habit of action. We fall into procrastinating. We become creatures of entropy.

This is one of the first things I work to correct with coaching clients. I work to see how quickly I can get them into the habit of taking action. With some it's about getting their action into a state of explosive efficiency, with others it's about rebuilding action and encouraging mindfulness in their thought patterns. It becomes about transitioning their thinking into tangible steps towards change.

DONE IS BETTER

Getting referrals is something every single one of my coaching clients will work on, no matter the level. It doesn't matter if they are a half million-dollar firm or encroaching on a $5 million firm. Referrals are going to be part of the program. When it comes to getting more referrals, there's a 'perfect' default many want to hit.

They want the perfect referral letter. They want the perfect campaign. They want the perfect newsletter. They want the perfect email or social media connection.

Perfect is the enemy of good. Moreover, perfect is the enemy of done. Done is better.

The first thing we have to do in improving referral marketing is figure out how to reach one person.

Just reach out to one person.
I dare you to do it.
Today.
Now.

Well, not literally now. Don't put the book down. Finish the chapter, then do it.

I dare you.

Reach out to one person you thought might make a good referral partner and find your in. Find the reason why you thought to reach out to that person and include it.

"Hey, I saw that you posted about such and such on LinkedIn. Thought it was really interesting. Would you be interested in a virtual or actual coffee together?"

It can change the trajectory way more than any thought you have. There will always be more reasons *not to do something.* All it takes to combat the legion of procrastination is the one reason in favor: **This may not get me there, but it sure will get me closer.**

A NEW VERSION OF YOU

You should always be on a road of personal growth. As your firm grows, and as you grow as a person, you should always be meeting the new version of you. This is one of the great journeys of the entrepreneur, and of the leader. You get to develop into the new version of you, over and over again. It's an exciting journey. As you become the new version of you, what "**Taking action**" looks like will change.

Actions look different as we grow as people, and as we grow the practices. Whether it's a direct hands-on action or the action of leading and delegating tasks, there are certain essentials to taking effective action. Don't be the person who knows the good idea and does nothing with it. Be the person who continually searches for great ideas and takes effective action with it.

This is where success is born. This is where it lives. This is kinetic energy. This is everything that propels great businesses forward. Mark Cuban doesn't become a billionaire because of his ideas. He does it by going out and selling those ideas. He does it by going out and executing. He takes action.

Today, start taking action according to where you are in the journey. If you have a smaller firm, you may personally be taking the action to crest your first seven figures. If you're starting to gain a lot of leverage through people in your practice, and setting expectations for how they should improve things, then you're taking action. Direct staff and fill in the tactics that they need to undertake to achieve the outcome you desire.

Everything is about the action that you take, the energy that you bring into this world. After all, you don't increase your fitness by sitting around and knowing a lot about fitness. You increase your fitness by doing something. There is a greater reward for the person who shows up and gets it done than the person who seems to know everything.

MAKE IT A HABIT

Once you start on the journey of being someone who takes action, make it a habit. That is what I am asking you to do. Be an action taker. Build that habit for yourself. Never be embarrassed to have done the 20%, because you are still farther along than others. I'll still ask you to try and hit your 100%. I wouldn't be a good coach if I didn't. What it really comes down to is effort and intention. It's a muscle. If you bring something, no matter the percentage, we can move the ball forward.

Keep building momentum. Be 50% of the person who is on the journey to their 100%. Be an action taker. Be kinetic.

Be right around the corner from the newest version of you.

ALCHEMY IN ACTION:

Take action: Rather than adopting an all or nothing mindset, be flexible with what you are able to accomplish and take action.

Done is better: Some action towards a goal is better than aiming towards perfection.

The new you: View yourself as a work in progress.

"JUST THE BEGINNING..."

HAVE YOU EVER come to the end of a major project and realized you were missing a critical component. This wrap-up chapter is a testament to this phenomenon, as I write it after deciding upon its existence right at the finish line.

This is my equivalent of the Seahawks choosing to run the ball instead of passing it at the goal line in Super Bowl XLIX. I'm not going to risk Malcom Butler pouncing on the route, nor will I let this book conclude without my final thoughts. It's the right and obvious choice.

Also, I'm a Denver Broncos and Detroit Lions fan. Yes, both. I was born in Denver, but I lived six fundamental years outside of Detroit during the Barry Sanders years.

Let's dispense with the football nonsense and get to the task at hand.

I dislike the way most people use business books. Too often, they are notches on the proverbial bedpost - a bragging right about how many you read.

If this book is just another number for you, that's too bad. You just received consolidated wisdom from over a dozen of the legal industry's top minds.

Every chapter has something you can do right now to improve your life and law firm. Plus, you just "met" all of those people and have a smorgasbord of new resources from which to choose - whether a company or new relationship to pursue.

I want you to DO SOMETHING.

There are plenty of ideas. You are now responsible for the actions.

I'll make a bold statement: if you could only do one or the other, I would rather you take action and change your life than tell anyone you read this book.

Sure, I'd love for you to tell others to pick up this book. However, it's more important to me that you take action. Turn all of this potential energy into the kinetic. Hire someone; launch a marketing campaign; dial in your data. Affect change in your life and law firm. Your transformation honors this book more than any review or referral to a new reader.

Of course, since we don't have to accept that binary, I wouldn't mind the review and referrals.

Let me ask...

What are you going to do?

If you need help focusing, I'll swipe Gary Keller's great question, "What's the One Thing such that by doing it everything else becomes easier or unnecessary?"

Take the action now.

I know I am drilling this home with the violence of Captain America wielding Thor's hammer - my favorite moment in all of the Marvel movies. However, it is my moral obligation to drill "take action" home. I will never forget a conversation with Mark Breyer, an 8-figure firm owner in Phoenix, when he left a mastermind group which I helped run. He was moving on not out of malice but because after 11 or so years, it was just time for him to seek another space. And he told me that over those 11 years, he saw one major difference between the members who succeeded and those who stayed stagnant. The successful ones actually did something with what they knew. Their talk results in a walk. And they never stopped walking, even when they fell down.

So here we are, my magnificent reader.

What are you going to do?

Choose something and just do it. You bought this book for a reason. And even if it was just to pad my numbers on Amazon (thank you, by the way), I implore you to do something with this book. I don't want to be just another number. I want us to change together.

Today's just the beginning of our next chapter.
Let's do big things together, shall we?

CLAIM $729 IN FREE RESOURCES
TO GET MORE CLIENTS, RECLAIM YOUR TIME, AND BUILD YOUR IDEAL LAW FIRM...

Add fuel to your entrepreneurial fire with our collection of guides, templates, and how-to information, guaranteed to help you:

- Generate high-quality, pre-sold leads for your law firm (so you can stop worrying about whether or not the phone is going to ring this week)

- Improve your leadership skills through superior communication techniques (which translate just as well to communication with a spouse or partner)

- Take back control of your marketing (including how to communicate with and hold your vendors accountable)

- Develop a stronger brand message (with a big, bold promise)

- Master your core financial numbers (so your firm runs like a well-oiled, profit-generating machine instead of a "what's happened lately" patchwork of decisions)

- And more!

This package of resources is exclusively for readers of this book, and to claim yours, just go to:

WWW.LAWFIRMALCHEMY.COM/VOLUME1

Go right now to get your hands on these free gifts for you!

ACKNOWLEDGEMENTS

MAKING A BOOK, much less a business, is far more fun to do with others than on your own. And I'm grateful to take this journey on with all of the folks below. Without you, this book doesn't exist.

The greatest gratitude is the easiest one. Thank you to Missy, the love of my life and best friend. We are still building a wonderful life together, even after 20 years of knowing each other, and 18 years together in love. I can hardly begin to show my total gratitude and affection for you. And how about those kids? Veronica and Cassidy, you girls are the best. Forever know Mom and I delight in all you do - with the exception of the bickering during bedtime routines. But that's just part of being siblings, isn't it? All of you provide the much-needed emotional energy and support to live out these entrepreneurial dreams. I love you.

Of course, I need to thank my team - the original pirate crew. Jenny Sajdera, it's remarkable how well we work together, covering totally different parts of our growing enterprises but with the same set of values and intentions. Your gifts and talents are immense. Thank you, thank you, thank you for building with me. Nonifel ("Ifhel") Balaba, my executive assistant, you are the organizational wizard who keeps me on track and sane (mostly - it's not an easy task after all). Bryan Austin, my high school friend and fellow theater kid turned collaborator, reuniting after all these years to make this new kind of art with me. Crazy how life worked out, right? Glad we're sharing a world again.

Tom Costello, Francine Costello, Jason Price, and the team at Word Association - your expertise in putting this book together has been invaluable. To Kia Arian and Kim McCann at Zine, thank you for dealing with the messiness of our design process, including more title alterations than should be legally allowed. It's amazing how much skill a person needs to make something seemingly simple actually look good.

Mom and Dad (aka Meg and Phil), thank you for letting me find my way. You clearly trusted in my ability to figure it out in life, even when I wasn't sure of the path. This gift of trust - including the insane decision to let me attend college as a theater major - is central to who I am today. Let's play some golf soon.

Next up, thank you to all the clients and customers of Law Firm Alchemy, especially members of our Genesis Mastermind and Catalyst Coaching programs. Keep chasing big lives!

Finally, this book would not exist without the incredible contributors who shared their expertise and insights. My deepest appreciation goes to:

Jan Roos, Andy Stickel, Kia Arian, Tony Albrecht, Len Spada, Tim Semelroth, Greg DuPont, Leah Miller, Cassidy Lewis, Ryan Mckeen, Moshe Amsel, Brandon Osterbind, Andrew Ayers, Emily Stedman, Kellam T. Parks, and Jessica Harrington.

If you found value in these pages, I urge you to seek out these contributors. Connect with them, follow their work, and pay close attention to what they have to say. Their insights extend far beyond these pages and continue to shape the legal profession in meaningful ways.

Lastly, I want to acknowledge you, the reader. You're freakin' awesome. This project is for you.

Cool...

Now I'm sitting here knowing there are so many other people I want to shout out. But I'm told this section can't list literally everyone.

So, here's my promise to you: if you think for a moment, "am I on Charley's personal list of gratitude," the answer is a huge YES. You are. I guarantee I've thought of you. Whether it's because you're numero uno (or one of the first) in becoming an LFA client or a compatriot who I see at legal events or a vendor who has referred clients to me... yes, I've thought of you. Thank you.

DON'T LET THE JOURNEY STOP HERE...

They Don't Teach This in Law School isn't just a book—
it's part of a bigger conversation that's been happening for years on our
podcast of the same name. This book was built from the powerful, raw, and
practical interviews we've had with real law firm owners who've faced the
same uphill climb you're on now—and figured out how to win.

Want more stories? More strategies? More behind-the-scenes
insight into how successful attorneys turned their practices into businesses
that serve their lives?

TUNE IN TO THE PODCAST.

Every episode gives you unfiltered access to the lessons no one's teaching
inside a classroom. It's the *ongoing education* you actually need to grow your
firm with clarity, confidence, and direction.

THIS BOOK IS JUST YOUR STARTING POINT.

The podcast is where the learning—and the momentum—keep going.

Search for "They Don't Teach This in Law School™"
on Apple Podcasts and Spotify.

(And don't forget to leave a 5-star rating and review while you're there!)

WA

www.ingramcontent.com/pod-product-compliance
Lightning Source LLC
Chambersburg PA
CBHW071549210326
41597CB00019B/3174